The Girl
Behind
the
Closed
Door

MARILYN AVIENT

1st WORLD
PUBLISHING

The Girl Behind the Closed Door

Marilyn Avient

© Marilyn Avient 2007

Published by 1stWorld Publishing
1100 North 4th St. Fairfield, Iowa 52556
tel: 641-209-5000 • fax: 641-209-3001
web: www.1stworldpublishing.com

LCCN: 2007930565
SoftCover ISBN: 978-1-4218-9978-7
HardCover ISBN: 978-1-4218-9979-4
eBook ISBN: 978-1-4218-9980-0

I dedicate this book to my mother,
Florence Harback.
*The road we have traveled together has
been sometimes rocky, sometimes smooth,
but always bordered on both sides with love.
Thank you for understanding that I
must do what I am called to do.
I love you, Mom.
(Don't worry about me anymore—I'll be OK!)*

*To Jason and Lindsey
Just because!
(I don't think your grandma will mind sharing
this page with you.)*

ACKNOWLEDGMENTS

I wish to acknowledge and thank the following people
for helping me make this dream come true:

John
For giving me your love along with a written lifetime guarantee.

Sean
Who knows what would have happened without you!

Special Thanks To
all the great people at 1st World Publishing
especially
Ed, Rodney, Mira and *Arwin*
"Oh—what you had to put up with!"

TABLE OF CONTENTS

Night after night,
she sat in her room all alone.
She knew that this was the only
place in her world
where she could be herself.
She had discovered that *they* liked
her to be happy, and so she was, when
she was out *there*.
But, *here*, she could think, and listen to
her favorite phonograph records.
Here she could cry about the boy who did not
like her, except as a friend.
Here she could cry from the sadness that
started way down in her toes.
Here she could wish that someone
would knock on the door—just to say "Hi."
Here she could daydream and imagine that
she was as pretty as all of her friends.
Here she could be the most popular girl
in the school.
Here she could imagine that she was
anyone else except

The Girl Behind the Closed Door.

Today,
The girl behind the closed door
Is very proud
Of the strong woman
I have become.

THE QUESTION IS ...

How can you know where you're going
If you don't know where you have been?
How can you remember your journey
If you are too blind to see what you've seen?
How do you know you've succeeded
If you've never been willing to fail?
How can you value air that is fresh
If you've never breathed air that is stale?
How do you know if something is good
If you've never seen anything bad?
How can you feel the wonder of joy
If you've never felt tearful or sad?
How can you take from your neighbor
What you've never been willing to give?
How can you say you'd be willing to die
If you've never been willing to live?

FEAR

This is a word that had ruled much of my life until I looked it square in the eye not too very long ago. I had *given* fear all the power that it had over me, and so I could also take it away. But first … I had to *own the responsibility* for having given away the best of me to this entity (that seemed larger than life in my eyes).

I was afraid of many things, and more afraid of the intangible than the tangible. I was afraid of what I could not see and what I thought I could not control. Physical possibilities such as someone breaking into my house did not evoke fear in me. Rather, I was afraid of my thoughts and feelings and of such things as the sound of the furnace coming on in the night (or what would happen if the furnace *did not* come on). My fears undoubtedly would have appeared foolish to anyone looking in from the outside, but to me, they were big; they were real; and they were all encompassing.

Fear is real, but it *is* a choice. I chose to feel fear twenty-four hours a day because of the pay-offs it had for me; I only felt alive when I was in its powerful grip and it was easy to get out of doing things if I said that I was scared to do them. While fear was an emotion that I said I hated, I was used to it, and was quite comfortable in its familiarity.

Today, I view fear differently. Now when I feel fear, I realize that I am edging close to something that scared me in the past for no rational reason. I now ask myself if this fear serves my life's purpose in any positive way, and if it does not, I try very hard to let it go. I take a moment to be gentle with myself, say a little prayer, and then I choose PEACE. What a marvelous feeling to finally know that I have the power to choose my feelings. There are many things I cannot control in this world, but I can control the way that I feel about them. I am the mistress of my own domain and it has only taken me half a century to figure that out!

FEAR

Somewhere deep inside of me
There's a little girl in tears.
She's afraid someone will hear her—
Merely one of many fears.
How can one so little
Be fearful of so much?
Is her fear the paralyzer
Or is it just a crutch?
Day after day, the panic grows
Within her tender breast.
She cries to God within her,
"Please, one hour of blissful rest."
The world out there is scary,
So hard, so cruel, so cold.
Little girls can make no choices,
They just do as they are told.
Sometimes she gets so tired
Just trying to keep ahead.
Fearing they'll discover her secret
Fills her little heart with dread.
To know what her Goliath is
Would make it possible to beat.
Faceless, nameless enemies
Are slow to fall in defeat.

THE HAVEN

One day I slipped away from them.
They knew not where I went.
I went inside to a place all mine,
My feelings all long spent.
I found a haven of darkness
So safe and so secure.
I felt so small and fragile,
Not one touch could I endure.
My being started to disappear,
I dared not close my eyes.
Slowly, slowly ... nearly gone.
Is this how a body dies?
With terror as my only friend,
I said, "Death would be best."
God smiled at me and shook His head,
"Not now, Child, get some rest."

THE CROSSROADS

Sometimes, in my mind I hear
A little voice at play.
It tells me to take chances,
To find another way.
My heart tells me to listen.
My mind says "Let it rest!"
I feel such mass confusion;
I fear to take the test.
I know I am at a crossroads
And only I can make the choice
Of whether to stay on the beaten path
Or turn and raise my voice.
A part of me says "Use the pain
and make good of your fight."
The other side, the little girl,
Is scared and says, "Take flight!"

THE LIE

I live in a world of fantasy
That reaches down to my very core.
I want to be so special
And do what's not been done before.
I want someone to see it,
But what happens if they do?
For only I know that I'm lying
And to the world, I am being untrue.
Just when I think I am being myself
My disguise becomes so plain.
One face I show to all the world,
But in the mirror, I see the pain.

Marilyn Avient

DEATH OF A FANTASY

I grieve, so deep, the fantasy
Of love, I thought was there.
I grieve the loss of people
With whom I thought my life I'd share.
Now, I know that what I want
Is not always what will be.
So many years it has taken
To teach my eyes to see.
I thought that I lived in a vacuum,
I thought that I was to blame.
With all the ills and pain that I've felt,
I, alone, acknowledge the shame.
Through all my years, I have been alone;
That, suddenly, now is plain.
The effort to feed my fantasy
Has yielded no freedom from pain.
But alas—the fantasy's buried!
I am free—I can make it alone.
The little child didn't deserve what she got,
For no sins has she to atone.
The people who want to be in my life
Have been there in sickness and health.
Now I can see the fortune I hold,
And reality's my greatest wealth.

A LITTLE GIRL IN PAIN

Originally, I wrote all of my poems by hand and then typed them using my old IBM Electra typewriter. Only years later did they find their way onto the hard drive of my computer. I am right-handed, but for this poem I used my left hand, which is supposed to stimulate the use of another part of the brain than that which is usually used. I believe that using my left hand reaches in and encourages the child in me to speak out. When I initiated this experiment, I had no idea what was going to come out, and this poem was the result. I know it refers to my father, who was my favorite person as a child, but I did not know that I, as a little girl, felt it to be so much work to love and be loved by him.

I know that this was definitely the child writing, because I, as the adult, do not remember having this depth of pain regarding my dad. I thought he was the one 'place' where I felt safely loved, but apparently not. Some of the language may sound a little too mature to have come from a child, but in this case it may have been possible because she was such a serious thinker, and well beyond her years in expressing her emotions within herself. This girl named Judy (I legally dropped that name in favor of my middle name, Marilyn, in 1996) was a very secretive child emotionally, and it took great courage to share these thoughts with anyone else—even me.

I treasure this poem because of that bravery, and because she trusted me enough to be honest. This indicates to me that healing is taking place. I have no doubt that letting her have the liberty of expressing her thoughts in this manner gave her the freedom to rid herself of even more of the hurts that have lived on in us right into adulthood. I am so proud of this little trooper who is such a vital part of me, and I know that Dad is smiling at her right now with the same love and pride that I feel.

A LITTLE GIRL IN PAIN

I'm just a little girl who tries very hard
To be what he wants me to be.
I'd move mountains to know of me he is proud,
For his smile, I'd push back the sea.
Why does he make me keep proving my love?
Why does he make my heart ache?
Why can't he see that I'm just a small child?
I wonder how much more I can take.
It hurts, how it hurts, when he keeps wanting more,
There's not much more left to give.
No matter how much, it's never enough.
For this lesson, God meant me to live.
I'll try very hard to be real good and kind
His pain is much bigger than mine.
I'll try very hard to love myself more
Maybe he'll love me more, given time.

THE CYCLE

I was actually surprised at the detail and emotion expressed in this piece that was written in about 1989. When I first re-read it a few months ago, I felt like I was reading and receiving this information for the very first time. I felt quite strange looking at this aspect of my life that was coming at me from the paper on which it was written. I felt like a deep dark secret was finally out of the bag. Every word of it was true and accurate, but it really looked foreign to me from the vantage point of wellness, which is where I am now.

I let my stepson, Andrew, read it during our letter writing years after he was deported back to Britain. [*More on Andrew later in the book.*] He said it was the best description of schizophrenia he had ever seen. That shocked me, because I had never entertained the thought of being seen as mentally ill to that degree. In my mind, depression was so far removed from schizophrenia that they should not be talked about in the same conversation.

What it did tell me, however, is that all mental pain is actually the same pain. It has just been given different labels depending on the presence or absence of a few differing outward symptoms. I thank God that I am now a long way from the everyday happenings described in this poem. And so it is.

THE CYCLE

The clouds are surely lifting to reveal a sun so bright.
The coolness of the shadows gives way to warmth of Light.
BUT ...
When darkness falls upon me
Mind creatures laugh and dance,
Making things seem so different
As though possessed or in a trance.
Darkness, the arch enemy,
Encloses me with bars;
Cuts off my sight of reality
And depletes the sky of stars.
Darkness fills my heart with fear, no freedom do I feel.
I see no differentiation—
What's fantastic—what is real?
Lurking in the shadows,
People hide and quake,
Disguised as loving and helpful, waiting for one mistake.
Flight becomes my only means
To really break away,
But legs of steel and a heart of fear force me here to stay.
If only they would stop laughing;
If only the noise would cease;
If only I could see some light;
My misery could I ease.

Then I awake one morning, happy and light of heart.
I know that I can conquer the world—
Other side of the cycle I start.
In Light, the smiles are friendly.
People are what they seem.
The darkness and the laughter
Are but elements of a dream.
In Light, mind creatures quiet down,
No bars around me stand.
The future lies before me
Like miles of sea and sand.
I wish I only could see the Light—darkness is no friend,
But it is the curse I carry
Perhaps 'til the day my life ends.

PAIN FROM THE PAST

Universe, I beseech you
To take these grievous thoughts.
Sprinkle them far unto the earth,
Let them fall on fertile ground.
I need them not; they hinder me
From being all that I can be.
They are a part of me that was,
But not of what will be.
Pain from a hurt remembered,
Not dealt with in its day,
Has fire and might as if it were new.
Let me feel it, then set me free

WHOLE IS A SUM OF THE PARTS

Lulubelle was a part of me for a very long time, and she is a topic big enough to fill a book all on her own. We occupied the same body while enduring a love-hate relationship that, from my point of view, was very difficult to handle at times. During my initial hospitalization in 1984, Lulubelle was a pivotal point when it came to doctors deciding how sick I really was. That was because for many years I was able to separate from her physically, and actually stand back and watch her in action. Because I was aware of the split when it was happening, the doctors called my condition *dissociation* as opposed to the more serious *multiple personality disorder*.

Lulubelle had come into my life when I was a small child because I needed to be the little girl that I thought the world needed me to be. Only she could make Dad laugh; a difficult thing to do at times because I think he suffered from his own kind of depression.

In my early adult years, Lulubelle was a social butterfly attracting men who would not have given me a second look on my own. When I no longer needed her and when I could no longer tolerate feeling inferior around her, I sent her away. Life was duller without Lulubelle because I was never able to match her daring and risk-taking ways again.

Now, years later, I see that she was a priceless, valuable part of me that I denied for a long time. At this point in my life, I could certainly use her talents, her enthusiasm, her mischief, and her unbridled lust for life. She was the fun side of me and sometimes I miss her. I would be happy to have her back because now I could handle her, and now I could love her. One day when I am in front of an audience, I know she will join me and I will greet her with open arms. At that moment, I will be complete. I will be whole.

WHOLE IS A SUM OF THE PARTS

Lulubelle with the laughing eyes,
So full of mischief and playful at heart.
A part of me I left in my past, but now, integration must start.
Her love she gave without question,
So easy, she was used in return.
She dared to balance her life on the edge,
And joke about Hell where she'd burn.
Lulubelle had another side,
She brought smiles when someone was down.
Many times, she entertained for hours on end,
Her name reflects how she felt like a clown.
Lulubelle didn't know the meaning of fear,
No need—I had both of our shares.
I cried, she laughed; I sighed, she sang,
Her whole world seemed devoid of all cares.
The battle surged on between us, but her presence
let me survive.
I hated the fact that he loved her!
Did he even know that I was alive?
Her fun, my guilt; her laughter, my tears
Became more than I could endure.
I went inside to a place that was mine—
Her death was my self-prescribed cure!
But how can I kill a part of myself
Thats as real as my hand or my face?
I tried to stifle her laughter; her beauty I tried to erase.

For many years I have lived my life,
The girl behind the closed door.
There has been a void within me,
where Lulubelle lived before.
Not she, who made him happy; nor she,
with talents galore!
It was me, who gave her power and charm,
It was me, who gave gifts and more!
Now Lulubelle stands before me,
I walk slowly—my hand, I extend.
She smiles as she sees my welcome,
I embrace her, my oldest friend!
Now we are one—the whole is me,
and together we'll face any foe.
I now feel free to be happy!
I now have the power to grow!

THE (WEEPING) WILLOW

There stands a tree, I know not where,
But I know she is just like me.
She stands alone on the top of a hill,
The world, for miles, she can see.
Not oak, nor birch, nor redwood,
But willow with limbs that can bend.
Her arms are long and far-reaching,
The earth she tries to befriend.
Around her lies a bed of grass
Interspersed with various weeds,
Who sometimes smile and say hello,
Then return to dispersing their seeds.
Below her stands a forest of trees,
A million heads that soar into space.
No time have they for the willow that bends
And lives in her own private place.
Who do you think could have planted that tree
So far from more of her kind?
God knew that He could force her to see;
In crowds, one tends to be blind.

HOPE

The day is fast approaching
When I shall grieve no more.
My heart shall open up windows
Instead of pounding on a closed door.

I have glimpsed the open waters
And heard the raging sea.
The echoes will not let me be content
To be less than I can be.

The tears I have shed are washing away
The bitterness and the fears,
But like the rain upon the rocks
The grinding-down takes many years.

I used to praise the setting sun
That signalled the end of the day,
But now I worship the sun that rises
And gives light to all I survey.

I had always liked the autumn best,
So jealous of leaves that could die.
Now I have felt the glory of spring
And my soul, reborn, yearns to fly.

The dark of night still follows the day,
The stars still bring on the sun.
In light or dark, my heart now feels safe,
Though not a child, my life's just begun.

Marilyn Avient

THE UNICORN

The unicorn saw he was different,
A horse, yet not, with a horn.
He wanted to fit in with the rest of the herd,
He wanted love, but instead he got scorn.
The magic inside him brought pleasure alone,
He thought he could share it outside,
But those who are born to be of this world
Think magic is better denied.
He tried and he tried to be one of them,
His efforts, it seemed, were in vain.
In daylight, he ran and played like a horse,
At night, all unicorn again.
When all by himself he would cry and loud curse
The horn that had set him apart.
He would rip and he'd tear at that monstrous thing,
Succeeding only at breaking his heart.
The sad would-be horse walked out to the sea
And let waves entice him to stay.
His tears mingled in with the water surround,
His cries, in the wind, died away.
The landscape is covered with horses,
No unicorns are seen on this Earth.
If only he had relished his oneness
And felt the blessing received at his birth.

FROM OUT OF MY KITCHEN WINDOW

In all of the other houses that I have lived in throughout my life, nothing has even remotely compared to the amazing view that I had from my kitchen window at South Cooking Lake. Every day I saw the fresh aftermath of the sun that was newly risen, and believe me, the ensuing peacefulness put a whole new slant on the mundane task of washing dishes! Over the years I saw moose, deer, rabbits, and many ducks and geese as I toiled over the kitchen sink.

To this day, I remember the feelings I had on those glorious mornings when I took the opportunity to enjoy the view even momentarily. When I was experiencing my 'craziest' days and refusing to sleep, I watched many a sunrise happening at the crack of dawn. For some reason, that sight always gave me a glimmer into the possibility that I was not depressed at the very core of me; in my Being. If I could still appreciate a beautiful sunrise, then there must be some hope that all was not lost.

Sadly, for me, that was one of only a few truly positive experiences that came from being in that house. I believe that I would never have survived, let alone have recovered, had we stayed there. I thank God for that wonderful view, and those fleeting moments of sanity that I felt because of it.

FROM OUT OF MY KITCHEN WINDOW

From out of my kitchen window I saw
The sun rise over the lake.
A ball of flames from out of the depths,
Preparing a new day to make.
No sounds, save birds, could be heard for miles.
The silence I heard was God's peace.
I stopped and worshipped when I saw a deer,
Its beauty, its truth—my release!
I saw a family of ducks on the lake,
Beyond them, I saw one alone.
I felt the tears well up in my eyes,
My heart quickly turned to stone.
I watched that duck swim quietly round,
No warning—he just flew away.
A piece of my soul chased him into the wind
To try to persuade him to stay.
I knew then that God had sent me a sign—
The duck, the deer—they were me.
He showed me that I, by myself, all alone
Would have the courage to set my soul free.

EULOGY TO ME

This poem was written at a time when I thought a lot about dying, but not necessarily at a time when I was suicidal. It was more a time when I was coming to grips with the fact that one day I would die, and my concern was that no one would remember me. I have kept this poem in my collection because it makes me feel gentle towards the girl behind the closed door who feared so much and trusted so few. She was weary of trying to be noticed, and tired of the never-ending job of trying to make people love her. She did not know that they just did, and she simply had to be present in order for that to happen. She worked so hard.

I read this now as though it was written by someone else, and that is good because it means I do not feel that way anymore. I now know that I am loved. I now know I am valued by many people and more importantly, I now value and love myself. One day a eulogy will probably be written about me, and it will involve many different things than are written here. It will say that:

🕯 I was a loving and generous mother, wife, and grandparent.

🕯 I was a colorful, eccentric, and ahead-of-her-time woman.

🕯 I was a poet, author, and innovative creator.

🕯 I was an honest and inspirational speaker.

🕯 I was a courageous searcher and teller of truth.

🕯 I was a wise and powerful counselor and confidante.

🕯 I was a spiritual person who recognized God in others.

🕯 I was a respected businesswoman.

I am a different person now than I was when I wrote the poem, but I love the woman-child who wrote it. God bless her now and always.

EULOGY TO ME

With outstretched arms, I take my leave
From my cares, my woes, my fears.
I am not alone; you need not grieve,
Do not remember me with tears.

I came to earth to do a task,
The lessons have been learned.
You gave me all that I did ask
Your love from me was earned.

When you remember my person
Think of me with a smile.
My journey has been a tough one
Covering many a lonesome mile.

Faithful, silent in the shadows
You waited caringly.
You gave me hope for meadows
You loved not sparingly.

Now I know the 'hows' and 'whys'—
The answers I've looked for.
Days now filled with blue skies,
My pain haunts me never more.

FREEDOM

FREEDOM is the will to live
To be all that I can be.
FREEDOM is having no control
Over all that I can see.
FREEDOM is the knowledge
That God's not in the sky.
He is a force within me;
Therein, my power does lie.

THIS DAY

A summer day in sunshine,
I want to see its light,
To feel the warmth of the morning sun,
And the coolness of the night.
I want to energize myself
To enjoy this day I am given.
I will not think of tomorrow
Until tomorrow's sun has risen.

JUST A LITTLE RABBIT

I saw a rabbit run out on the street
My car lights shone in his eyes.
I saw the terror within him
As he pictured his own demise.
No doubt he was lost, away from his kin,
No safety, no place could he hide,
A world where there was no place for his kind,
A world where Nature's defied.
My heart went out to this rabbit,
I wanted to show him I care.
I wanted to take the fear from his eyes
And carry him home to his lair.
I cannot forget the terror I saw
Nor this creature so lost and alone.
A city has no time for caring
With heart made of concrete and stone.

A LITTLE GIRL IN ORANGE SOCKS

I will never forget this day. I dare to surmise that some other forces were at work in me that day because this event has now taken on a mystical quality in my mind. I can still hear the child's voice echoing through time and space. I can see those socks of orange that stand out in my memory as shining like the brightest sun, and being just as important as anything I have seen before or since.

I guess it is that way because, in essence, I was seeing and hearing a little girl from the past. She feels mystical in my mind because the girl I was remembering would never have called out like that for the entire world to hear. She certainly would never have worn anything so lively or adventurous as those neon orange socks. Those socks would have made the child that was me stand out in the world and be visible, and that would not have been endured. As a child I felt invisible and solitary and that became my comfort zone. The little girl in the field who was wearing the orange socks was all I wished I could have been. She was worldly. She was visible. She was uninhibited.

This was an instance when I felt overwhelming love for someone whom I did not know, and whose face I could not see. I loved the essence of her voice, I loved her energy, and I loved her choice in clothing. I had never felt that way before, and it was an experience of my soul that I will cherish always. I just had an image flash before me of the girl behind the closed door daring to wear orange socks in the safety of her own little haven, and looking quite proud of herself for doing it.

God bless both of these little girls.
Each is a treasure in her own right.

Marilyn Avient

A LITTLE GIRL IN ORANGE SOCKS

A little girl in orange socks
Went skipping across the field.
I watched her from the top of a hill,
From her, my presence concealed.
To me, she looked so tiny,
I just sat and watched her run.
She called and called another child's name,
Her orange socks gleamed in the sun.
I could not see her face at all,
So far was she from me.
I giggled when she spun cartwheels,
Her little heart seemed so carefree.
I do not know what happened next,
My eyes suddenly burned with tears,
My vision became like a tunnel,
She became a child who had been gone for years.
A child who yearned to run in the field,
To spin cartwheels, just for the fun,
To mindlessly scream out into the wind
And wear socks that gleamed orange in the sun.

INSOMNIA

I am writing a comment on this poem because, for some reason, I remember clearly the night that I wrote it, which is not the case with many of my poems. I remember sitting alone in our condo at about midnight and feeling so powerful that I thought I could do absolutely anything that I set my mind to doing. What a marvelous feeling that was! I sat there glowing in the peace of knowing my own capabilities. I did not want to forget the feeling and so I wrote this poem.

What is not said in the poem is that this feeling happened often and always at night when it was difficult to put action into play. I could sit and dream, but the whole world was at rest, so I could do nothing else about it. I did not need to put action onto my thoughts and that was why I dared to think them.

I have finally figured out the methods behind the way I did things. All day long, at that time in my life, I was gripped with fear and, in effect, was paralyzed by all the unknown forces that I knew were out to get me. I was afraid of committing to anything because what if my depression returned? I was afraid of telling possible future employers, in a job interview, that I could do certain tasks because what if I could not? I was afraid of succeeding at anything because what if they figured out that I was a fraud? In the light of day, I was committed only to my fears and nothing else. In the safety of darkness, I could dream to my heart's content. Rarely, I would even go so far as to take my ideas to bed, and predictably, by morning they were smashed into unrecognizable pieces that had no hope of being reassembled.

Now I dream by day, and then I act on that dream. Some dreams are just for the pleasure of dreaming, while others are the starting points for ideas that are growing into my life's work. I like to think that those dreams of fifteen years ago were the seeds that have now grown into fledgling plants. I will never let myself see any phase of my life as having been a waste—it was just a part of the process that is ME.

INSOMNIA

Around me falls the silence
Of a house prepared for sleep.
My mind responds in defiance,
Wakefulness, it yearns to keep.
Youth and hope permeate my heart,
With a feeling of blissful control.
Unbound excitement, not a small part
Of the happiness now in my soul.
How can I lie on my pillow and dream
When here and now I can conquer the world?
My head is full of many ways and schemes
That by morning will all be unfurled.
Daybreak deflates me with power and might,
While the night, it lights up my heart.
Moonbeams and gentle starlight please stay.
I beg you, don't let the day start.

SO, A FLOWER HAS NO SOUL

This poem was written to honor the people of society who do not have recognizable value. They may be drug addicts, convicts, homeless persons, schizophrenics, or anyone who has slipped through the cracks into obscurity. I saw a movie starring Nick Nolte called *"Weeds"* about a group of ex-convicts who made good. They likened themselves to the weeds that grow between the cracks or that people pick from their gardens and throw away in disgust. I thought of my stepson, Andrew, and how he was always somewhere that he should not have been, and how he just never seemed to fit in with the rest of us.

All of these 'dispensable' people have souls and are loved by God just as much as Mother Teresa, Martin Luther King, or you and I. They just look different, act different, and have a different perspective on the world. Many of us are very quick to judge other people on the basis of their actions, without ever bothering to consider their spirits. On a soul level, we are all equal—we have all just chosen different lessons to learn. What if these "weeds" are just younger souls who have not had the time to master as many lessons as the more mature ones?

Since writing this poem and seeing the movie, I have looked differently at the weeds of nature. What I have found when I am really looking, is that these weeds are filled with beauty. However, there is a great abundance of some of them and they propagate without inhibition. I wonder if that is what eliminated them from the garden flower category—they were just too free in their actions and they refused to be tamed and contained by people who did not have their best interests at heart.

SO, A FLOWER HAS NO SOUL

They say a flower has no soul;
So from where does its beauty come?
Too much credit is given to watering
And just the right place in the sun.
But what of the seed that falls in a crack
Between slabs of concrete and stone?
It forces its way up into the light
And thrives there all on its own.
The woodlands are filled with wild flowers
That live in the shade of the trees.
Their beauty goes unnoticed,
They are ignored by all but the bees.
Some flowers are shunned and destroyed at will,
We, men, have called these plants "weeds."
No soul, no mind, the weeds fight back
By dispersing a myriad of seeds.
No matter where a flower grows
Its beauty, unblemished, unfolds.
The tainted, imperfect semblance of man
Must reflect the pain of our souls.

DENIAL

How can something so distant
Be the continuing cause of pain?
Slipping away to the recesses,
Then returning to haunt again.
Pain cannot be buried
Just because you wish it were dead,
As long as you keep it hidden,
Pain gathers new life and dread.

SILENCE OF THE SONG

I hurl my voice out into the wind,
But, alas, I hear no reply.
I yell and I scream to the rooftops,
My echoes bounce back from the sky.
I wonder aloud where can they all be,
The crowd has just left me alone
To face the confusion within me,
To face the world on my own.
The world at large goes forging ahead
And thinks I am tagging along.
My ears have gone deaf to its music,
My soul plays a singular song.
So why do I think they should listen to me
When I, in fact, pay no heed
To the stirrings that I hear within me;
So afraid of where they may lead.
Perhaps my mouth never opened,
Perhaps I'm just screaming inside!
The noise within me has silenced my song
And, hence, I remain fortified.

WHO SHALL FLING THAT FIRST STONE?

This poem was written after hearing the judgments that various people had made about my stepson, Andrew, who was addicted to hard drugs and various painkillers. He was a very intelligent person who made many choices that eventually led to his death at 33 years of age. Underneath the drugs was a boy in pain, and even though we chose not to live with that boy on a daily basis, we loved him and knew that deep down inside, he was a good person. Unfortunately, Andrew only let that goodness be seen on rare occasions, and thus, many people judged him and were unwilling to see him in any other light than that of the "useless druggie." I know this saddened and embarrassed his father, my husband, very much.

In 1989, Andy was deported back to Britain and lived in London, England until his untimely death. For three years, we carried on a friendship by mail, and I am so glad I had that opportunity to get to know him in ways that could only evolve in the safety of being miles apart and putting pen to paper. About six months before his death in 1994, he stopped phoning—which he had done from a public payphone—and he stopped answering my letters.

I wrote this poem in 1992 and he died in 1994. This was my reaction to some of the comments I heard about this 33 year old "boy" whose body just gave up one day after too many years of self-abuse. His ashes were scattered off the summit of Mount Lady MacDonald in Canmore, Alberta. Once airborne, these last physical remnants of our son flew into a pass used by large birds in their migratory flight path. When we saw that, we smiled because Andy was doing in death what he could not do in life—he was flying with the eagles!

Marilyn Avient

WHO SHALL FLING THAT FIRST STONE?

To judge another human being
For words uttered or actions done,
Is declaring yourself the winner
Even before the race has begun.
No one is given exemption in life,
Temptations will darken our way.
No one has truly the foresight to know
Just what he will do on that day.
I believe there are two kinds of people,
Who no mercy to others can show.
The action, so cruel, is the judgment,
Their motive—only they know.
The first of the two is the Earthbound saint
Whose life is enclosed in a shell.
He prays and worships at an altar of fear
And condemns other men into Hell.
The other judge is dishonest (at best),
He uses others to pay for his shame.
He sees his own actions and thoughts in their deeds,
He suffers—let them do the same!
Fret not; there still are some people
Who never would fling that first stone.
They listen with hearts of compassion and know
It's not for them to condemn or condone.
Innately, there are no bad people,
But there are many who stumble and fall.
One kind word may give them the courage to stand,
But judgment will force them to crawl.

WORLD FULL OF PAIN

Sometimes, I think I am giving my all,
I think I am doing my best.
I worry about the fact that I'll fail
When I haven't even taken the test.
I think that I am stretching my arms,
But all I have reached for is me.
It's time to step right out of myself,
I may be surprised at what I will see.
Beyond myself, I see a world
Too vast to comprehend;
Addictions, disease, and poverty
And attitudes that will not bend.
I see children who go to sleep in tears
And mental patients in constant pain.
I see people who hide within themselves
And refuse to acknowledge their shame.
I see people who grieve for loved ones,
And others who fear to grow old.

Then I look and see countless thousands
Who lose themselves in the quest for gold.
Alas, but I could go on and on
At the havoc Man does to himself.
I could rant, I could rave and show my disgust
And claim innocence all for myself.
But no, I am guilty—more guilty than they
For I sit and I watch and I wait.
I see the pain and do nothing to help,
My kind of love could be likened to hate.
So now I must reach way deep down inside
And find the gifts that I have to give.
If I don't give something to my fellow man
What reason do I have to live?

POWER OF THE FULL MOON

Just when I see the progress I've made,
A moon so full lights the sky.
It tugs like a weight on my heartstrings,
My wings refuse to fly.
The moon with childlike innocence
Has power, not seen, on my heart.
In silence, it distributes a magic
That unmercifully pulls me apart.
The sun is given the power of kings
To warm and light up our souls.
On cloudy days we feel less alive,
In sunshine we strive for our goals.
The moon, however, receives no respect,
Thus slighted, revenge it does seek.
In darkness, the mouse is a lion,
Full moon, the lion feels meek.

Marilyn Avient

I MUST REMEMBER I AM LOVED

Just when I thought I would fall to the depths
I was rescued by people who care.
I was feeling like I was alone on the earth,
My proverbial cupboard felt bare.
My children reached out to touch me,
They begged me not to fall.
They reached down deep within themselves,
They answered my stifled call.
They said that they were giving to me
The lessons I had given to them.
Their words—my tears—gave rise to hope
And myself I could cease to condemn.
I am blessed with family who love me,
A fact I choose to forget
When I let myself slide out of the Light
And into the dregs of regret.

MOMENT OF AWARENESS

I feel a pressure so heavy—
Injustice—each direction I turn,
Weighing me down with intensity
That increases the more that I learn.

What can I do to change a world
Blind and deaf with no ears or eyes?
Blindly, recklessly forging ahead
No effort its ills to disguise.

Awareness is creeping out of my soul
Slowly filling the void in my heart.
I feel the need to do something,
God help me—where do I start?

Answers are held by the Universe
It knows what needs to be done.
It knows what can be accomplished
By a crowd that adds up to one.

Let not this feeling desert me;
For once, I am feeling alive.
I ask You to give me direction,
To Your goodness, I promise to strive.

JUST WHEN I THINK ...

Just when I think I am one of a kind
And liken myself to a saint,
I get a humbling that knocks me off stride
And makes me beg for restraint.
I walk around with my nose in the air
And give advice to all whom I see.
I fool myself and I fool the world
That I am truly the best I can be.
I've tried to please the whole world at large
And make them think I am the best,
But lessons of worth are seen by just me,
At times I do not pass the test.
Only I know where my weaknesses lie
And I know how to keep them from view.
I've hidden away in hope of control
Keeping shame from shining through.
I have a lesson that needs to be learned
I will keep at it 'til I get it right.
One flaw has haunted me since my dawn
And its repair may take until night.

A GIFT OF PEACE

In 1992, I was working as an assistant to an angel in my life named Reggie. Tired of the usual cards available at Christmas, she asked me to write a poem that she could send to clients, friends, and family. Even though I had much to be grateful for that year— John survived a heart attack and surgery—all of my frustrations and hurts about this annual holiday season came out full-tilt in this poem. Reggie liked it, however, because it was truthful, and not soft and shallow as many seasonal poems are.

I have always had a problem with Christmas being portrayed as this magical time when families dress up in fancy clothes and gather around a tree to sing carols. That is the scene that the media has chosen to depict a 'normal family' at Christmas, but what about those people who have no families? What about the families who are so troubled and burdened with pain that they do not know any joy? What about the families who have no money for the velvet dresses, presents, or eggnog? What about the family around whom this holiday is supposed to be celebrated?

I am tired of the commercialization of Christmas and feel that it should be a private day to be celebrated, or not, depending on one's own personal belief system. Everyone has to decide what this season really means on a spiritual level. That is difficult because we have become bogged down with the surface traditions of trees, and holly, and lights. This poem helped me deal with my feelings, and thus, put many of them to rest. More importantly, the expressing of my inner thoughts on paper made me feel authentic in my own eyes. Any poem that can do that has to be worth something!

A GIFT OF PEACE

Christmas is more than holly and snow
And tinsel embellishing a tree.
Christmas is more than giving out gifts
To people you so rarely see.
Christmas is more than going to church
One night out of all of the year.
Christmas is more than hearts full of joy—
It often means hearts full of tears.
Christmas is more than family love
When so many poor souls are alone.
Christmas is more than words from a Book,
Whose stories, since a child, you have known.

Christmas is when you look into your heart
And see a love that is real and alive.
Christmas is when you're discouraged and lost,
But still you continue to strive.
Christmas is when you reach into your soul
And give yourself to your fellow man.
Christmas is when you feel love, joy, and hope
Because you know that you're a part of the Plan.
Christmas is when you look neither forward nor back,
But are happy to be here in the Now.
Christmas is when you neither worry nor fret,
For you know that you'll make it somehow.

We all hope at Christmas that this is the year
When finally our hearts will know love.
We wish for the magic that stories relate
Is our inherent gift from above.
How can one day be the answer to dreams?
How can all that we wish for come true?
If we put the same effort into each of our days
There'd be no limit to what we could do.
So instead of wishing you "Merry Christmas,"
I'll wish you peace for each day of your life.
Then you'll have a gift with each rising sun,
And soon joy will replace all your strife.

MY FUTURE

The lacy patterned paper shines
Beneath satin ribbon and bow.
I see my name upon the card,
The contents, I yearn to know.

As it sits, it holds the world—
Excitement fills my every pore.
Will it be a total surprise
Or something I have thought of before?

I have the choice to rush right in
To tear the paper and ribbon apart,
Or I can sit and fantasize
And dream it will please my heart.

As long as it remains untouched
Who knows what the gift could be—
Like gold or frankincense or myrrh
Or mermaids from out of the sea.

The lacy patterned paper shines
Beneath satin ribbon and bow.
For now the mystery is my gift,
Someday, its essence I'll know.

HOW DO YOU KEEP ON DANCING?

How do you keep on dancing
When it seems that the music has died?

How do you learn to laugh at yourself
When since birth, at yourself you have cried?

How do you teach your eyes to see light
When they're conditioned to greyness and black?

How do you see a cup that's half full
When before, you've just seen what it lacks?

How do you know what you're doing is right
When you've thought all along you were wrong?

Why do you keep believing you're weak
When those around you keep saying you're strong?

I must open the doors to the house of my soul
And hear music that only I hear.

I must see myself with the humor of youth
And laugh in the face of my fear.

I must look inside until I see my light
And know that it's shining from me.

I must look in the cup and acknowledge what's there
And not grieve what's not there to see.

I must have the faith that I'm being led
And know that for me it is right.

I must take a look at all that I've done
And believe that I've fought a good fight.

NO ONE IS LISTENING

Have you ever heard a pin drop
As it crashes to the floor?
Have you ever heard a foghorn
Though it be miles away from shore?
Have you ever heard a heart beat
In someone else's chest?
Have you ever heard a wave break
As the shore kisses every crest?

All so quiet—yet all have been heard.
All so minor—yet you were stirred.

So why can no one hear me
From so deep, my soul does scream!
Perhaps I am invisible ...
And my pain ... just one bad dream.

IN SEARCH OF SERENITY

I want to find Serenity;
Can you show me the way?
North or South or East or West?
Should I arrive by night or by day?
I have walked down many paths in life,
But none have taken me to this place
Where my heart can play in the morning sun
And at night, sleep in its own special space.
In Serenity, there are no watches or clocks,
No appointments or things to be done.
No one will tell me what I should be doing
No work, no demands—only fun!
In this place where I long to be,
I'll call the squirrels and ducks by name.
The birds will chirp their awareness of me,
Wild creatures, to me, will be tame.
In Serenity, there are no clouds of grey,
Just white billows in a sky so blue,
And in this place, no rain will fall.
God gives moisture in the form of dew.
Is there a place like this on Earth
Or is it a dream of the very best kind?
I think if I want this freedom of heart,
I must create such a place in my mind.

I WISH THAT I COULD GO SOMEWHERE

I wish that I could go somewhere
And hide myself away.
I would sit and watch the sunrise
Then do as I please all day.
No cares, no fears, no problems,
My heart could take over my head.
The sun would soothe me with its warmth
And stars would stand guard o'er my bed.
Cheerful, singing songbirds
Would trill and I would know
That I was in the house of God
Where there is refuge and peace for my soul.
No matter where I chanced to look
I would see flowers blooming bright,
Each feeling so important
Because God surrounded them with Light.
The sky would be a tranquil blue
Punctuated with clouds of cream,
I would lie on a bed of silken grass
And sigh—like in a dream.
The clouds would all be figures
Of whatever I chose them to be.
A galloping horse or a handsome prince;

My eyes could see what they wanted to see.
I would romp with glee in the meadows,
My arms would reach out for the sun.
The animals would come out of hiding,
One by one, they would join in my fun.
Inside me I would feel the child
Who had freckles and short brown hair.
I would stop and smile when I heard her laugh,
Now happy and free from care.

LESSON #593
BUT THEN WHO'S COUNTING?!

This is quite a 'snotty' little poem. I had been a martyr all my life and I only felt alive when I *thought* I was carrying someone else's burden for them. Now I know that that is not possible to do because we each have our own load, and it is not in my power to relieve anyone of his or her pre-planned lessons. However, I really thought I could, and I think the motive behind my madness was the notion that if I relieved them of their pain, then they would love me—simple as that.

I worked with a woman whose son died in a farming accident. Although I had never met him, she would talk to me about her loss and all of the family problems that followed it. After I had said all that I could to comfort her and help her, I decided on some level that the only *real* way I could help would be to take the pain from her. Before long, I found myself grieving for this son that was not mine, and I found myself thinking about him as though he were. I became so sad and yet, I remember feeling like an outside observer watching the two of us interact. How could she still be feeling so bad, when I thought that I had taken the pain from her? I ended up in hospital not too long after that, because I guess I had done this little stunt one time too many, and it just was not working. I had taken on too many sorrows that were not mine, and I could not handle the agony anymore.

Sometimes the situation would involve someone telling me of their financial woes, and this would cause me to stay up nights fretting about the difficulties as though they were mine. I have taken on other people's problems of all sizes, and of all varieties, and, miraculously, the writing of this poem stopped much of it. I do not remember the exact incident that triggered the writing, but it must have been a showstopper. Now all the energy I expended on everyone else is mine, and there is beautiful freedom in that.

LESSON #593
BUT THEN WHO'S COUNTING?!

I, alone, must live my own life
And you, my friend, must live yours.
The windows of life are open to all,
We must search to find our own doors.
In times of joy, it is easy
To claim our lives as our own,
To accept and acknowledge successes
As seeds entirely self-sown.
When stress and strain come into our worlds
The story is not quite the same.
So often we spread the poison we feel
In hopes of sharing the blame.
If you have a weighty problem, dear friend,
I will listen and comfort your pain.
I will not accept what is rightfully yours,
The burden is yours to retain.
A lesson I am learning half-way through my life
Is becoming so perfectly clear.
I cannot carry your sorrows and grief,
At most, I can lend you an ear.

THE SEEDLING

Her memories of him are stained
By hordes of falling tears.
I wish that she could tell me
Of her joys, her pain, her fears.
Too small she was—too fragile
To have to be so strong.
So smart she was—so crafty
She righted every wrong.
This girl adored her daddy,
They were close, but didn't know
Seedlings need the air to breathe
With space between each row.

Marilyn Avient

LIKE BRUTUS AND CAESAR

A fond farewell I bid you,
I thought you were my friend.
Those days and nights you spent with me—
Who'd have thought they would ever end.
You were always there beside me,
No matter—snow, or rain, or shine.
I needed you, or so I thought,
Like a vagabond needs his wine!
My friend, you were the important one,
I would have given my life up for you.
Behind my back you were laughing
Because that is just what you meant me to do.
But now those days are over,
I don't miss you like I thought that I would.
I admit I'll never forget you;
Best you left while the memories were good.
The world sees me now with kinder eyes.
Each day, brighter the sun seems to get.
Perhaps it's my mind that is brighter
Without you, my old friend, Cigarette!

AGAINST THE TIDE

The waters of the river flow
So naturally to the sea.
This plan of Nature says, "Start small,
Then grow as big as you can be."
Who is Mother Nature anyway
And why is she so smart?
My plans are born as big as oceans
And there my journey starts.
I jump into my leaky boat
And paddle fiercely against the tide.
I, soon, am discouraged and weary,
My boat gets tossed from side to side.
Not long, I see I am ill-prepared
For perils I need to face,
One tiny oar to beat the waves,
No rhythm, no well-planned pace.
I pass the boats who are heading to sea,
They wave and wish me well.
They look like they're going to Heaven
While I feel like I'm going to Hell.
Sometimes I dare to put down my oar
To see how far I have come.
I am no closer to where I am going
And just barely past where I am from.

Marilyn Avient

My boat is filling with water,
I fear that it will sink.
Between bailing out water and fighting the tide,
There's no time for me to think.
When all my strength has left me
I lie down and hope to die.
"You failed again," my mind does say,
"So why do you even try?"
I think of the boats who passed me
That looked so wise and so serene.
They seemed to know where they were going
While I hardly know where I've been.
I came to this earth to learn to be me.
If I don't accept me, who will?
I fight the tide because that's who I am
And when I'm dying, I'll be fighting it still.

THE COLD WIND

I hear a cold wind calling me,
No place is there to hide.
The name I hear is mine alone,
In fear, I crawl inside.
The sun outdoors is blazing hot,
Its glare is blinding red.
I feel no warmth; I see no light,
I shiver with chills of dread.
I curse and grieve these winds of fate
That blow and call me by name.
I curse and grieve these winds of fate
That use my soul as a pawn in a game.
I guess that I had been feeling too warm
And forgot that ice does exist.
Perhaps I've been humbled and brought back to earth
By lessons too strong to resist.
The freezing wind howling at my heart
Made me stop and listen awhile
To messages sent by the Universe
That prepared me to walk the next mile.

A FRIEND

A friend is one who knows
A door can open in or out.
A friend is one who shares her thoughts
With ease and with no doubt.
A friend is one who cares enough
To take and then to give.
A friend is one who knows the words
To make the other want to live.
A friend is one who trusts in love
And says, "Please hold my hand."
A friend is one who smiles with love
And says, "I understand."

ODE TO A FRIEND

Some persons in a lifetime
Stand out amongst the rest.
She was one I called a friend.
To me, she was the best.
In days when darkness covered me
I would look and she'd be there.
She gave to me of her own strength,
I questioned why she'd care.
Why did she care what happened to me
When others fell to the side?
In her, I knew a safety.
In her, I could confide.
One day she stood at my bedside,
I begged her to take me home.
She cried and felt so helpless
As she watched me turn to stone.
She thought that she could cure me.
She did all that was right.
She thought that she could lead me
From the darkness to the Light.
Tricks she tried, to show me
That my life was of some use,
But she could not feel inside me
Or understand the self-abuse.

One day I said that I must die
To make the pain go away.
Angry, hurt, frustrated, she said,
"I'm sorry. I cannot stay."
In time, love won over anger.
In time, my soul did heal.
She learned that one can't heal another
'Though the desire to do so is real.
The clouds have left my horizon—
I had to send them away.
The love she gave is one of the things
I'll remember on my dying day.

A MOMENTARY FRIEND

This poem was inspired by a woman whom I met while sitting on a bench at a bus stop in 1990. In 1989, I had decided to conquer one of my long-standing fears and so I went to university. I lasted only one year, but it was a year of great learning, and not all of it came from books and lectures.

On this particular day, I was more stressed out than usual, which is really saying something because I was the queen of stress at that time. Sometimes I wonder how my heart has held out over the years with the amount of panic and the number of adrenalin rushes that it has endured. My perfectionism and insistence that I outshine every other person on Earth really reared its ugly head during that short stay in the halls of higher education. I studied every waking minute and received top grades in everything I did. I quit at the end of one year because I did not have the courage to accept a less than perfect grade, which was bound to happen eventually. I know the folly of my ways now, but still, have never returned to complete my degree.

I think that the woman on the bench was an angel sent to me just to lull me with her silken speech. As soon as we met we talked about very deep spiritual topics and I was glad the bus was late that day. By the time it arrived, I felt more peaceful than I had felt in a very long time. I never saw her again and to this day, I think she was there just for me. She probably saved me from having a heart attack because I felt out of control when I first sat down, and I was calm and peaceful when I got on the bus. Whoever you are, wherever you are, I thank you. God bless.

Marilyn Avient

A MOMENTARY FRIEND

Won't you come and sit awhile,
For now, you and I could be friends.
My heart and my soul, I will share with you,
Your wisdom to me, would you lend?
The path I walk gets lonely
And I crave a friendly face.
I love to hear your voice of silk,
Your presence to me is a grace.
Shall we stop for a moment and ease our loads,
And look about us at the wonders surround?
The flowers smile at us their beauty,
We sigh at the magic we've found.
For one short moment I lean on you,
Your strength and wisdom I gain.
You look at me; I feel your respect,
My weariness like a faucet does drain.
It's time to go, our paths diverge,
We each must make our own way.
With strength anew I head out alone
I thank you, my friend, for this day.

THEY COME AND THEY GO

I wrote this poem at a time when people seemed to be making entrances and exits non-stop in my life. Some people would break my heart when they left; with others, I would just notice one day that they were gone with no goodbyes and no fuss nor muss. Still other people have come into my life just when I needed their particular talents or gifts, and they seemed to appear just as soon as I expressed that need. I love it when the Universe gives me a sign that I am a part of the Plan!

Those who leave easily and unnoticed have small but vital tasks to do, and then they go. Those with more impact will leave a bigger hole upon departure. I have also considered that my reaction to their leaving may be the lesson in and of itself.

I am always interested in how a person arrives in my world. I love it when I meet someone apparently new and we connect immediately like the oldest of friends—which we probably are on a soul level. I am also interested when I meet someone to whom I take an immediate dislike. I have actually met people who have said nothing to me more complicated than "Hello" and I have had the urge to punch them right in the face. A strange feeling, but I am grateful that I do have some sense of decorum, because I manage to restrain myself on such occasions. Thankfully, I usually do not see much of them again, but I am always taken aback when such a reaction comes over me.

All I know for sure is that every person who crosses my path has a purpose on a soul level that I may never understand on a physical one. I planned that purpose so I cannot complain about it, or conversely, congratulate it too loudly. I just have to live with it and try to make worthy choices with these persons who eventually affect my life on all levels.

Marilyn Avient

THEY COME AND THEY GO

I see the persons, who pass through my life,
Some stay, some go, some pass out of sight.
Each has a purpose; a role to fulfil;
Some roles are large, while others are slight.
My soul chose the parents, from whom I could learn,
And siblings who would share in my youth,
My husband, my partner in braving the world,
My children who make me face truth.
The people are chosen who will make me less blind,
To see life as it is through my eyes.
Not all the sights will be pleasant to see,
But each in its turn makes me wise.
Some folks pass through like a whisper,
They come, leave their gift, and they go.
So quiet, I may miss what they've given,
But later think back and I know.
So often I grieve the loved ones I've lost
And question the plans of my soul.
One day I will learn the lessons I'm taught
By entities beyond my control.
Some people come and some people go,
No meeting is ever by chance.
No matter the nature of gift that they give,
My life, in the end, they enhance.

LIKE PLANTS OR FRIENDS

Sometimes we become quite lethargic about tending to the needs of our friendships, just as we neglect our plants in the midst of our busy schedules. This was happening with someone very dear to me and so I wrote her this poem. I do not think that it changed anything for her, but at least I got it off my chest. Now I just have to accept that our friendship happens when it happens and that is okay.

I am as guilty as anyone else about not being attentive to all of my friends all of the time. I also know that I am often the instigator of getting together, and sometimes I tire of always having that role. However, since this pattern has hit many areas of my life, I have decided to call myself a leader, and that makes it feel like an entirely different situation indeed.

Life is fragile, as is obvious, when one is handling a delicate flower or trying to catch a butterfly. Life is fragile when dealing with the feelings of others and sometimes, even when our intentions are well-meaning, we hurt people with our robust enthusiasm. Neglect is another form of abuse, and so if we put off seeing someone long enough, (even if we think that person will be there for us no matter what we do) we may be in for a surprise. I may love someone unconditionally; however, if I am treated badly, I may have to leave. That does not affect the way I feel about that person; it just means I do not accept the neglect any longer.

How common it is to wish we had been more attentive to someone after that person is gone. If only we had felt those sentiments while he or she was still with us. So many cases of guilt could be eliminated if we were to just stop once in a while, and remember how important people are in our lives. It takes only a moment to call and say "I love you!" It takes a very long time to get used to them being gone.

LIKE PLANTS OR FRIENDS

A relationship, any relationship
Is a living, breathing thing.
Just as a favorite plant in
Your garden cannot grow
Without sunshine, water, nutrients and love,
So, too, do the people in your life need care.

A child who gets too little love and attention
Fails to thrive, then dies.
A spouse who is not made to feel special or
Who is taken totally for granted,
One day leaves
With shriveled heart in hand.

A friend, like the plant, is beautiful.
A friend, like the child, is fragile.
A friend, like the spouse, has a heart.
A friend is different because
She can survive with less.
A friend is the same because
She cannot be taken for granted
And one day she, too, will die.

LETTING GO

I am constantly amazed by the no-nonsense approach that I have put into some of the poems in this collection. In this particular poem, I think I had to sound strong, and I had to sound tough, in order to make me feel like I could actually do what I had to do. I was a control freak and I could not imagine life without knowing every detail of my sons' lives. I wanted to protect them from pain and difficult things, which is not only impossible, but also not fair, because it means cheating them out of some wonderful lessons.

I must have gotten myself involved in some details of their lives that I really did not want to be in, and so I had to make a clean break, if only in my mind and on this paper. I did it by sounding much tougher than I really was and it worked in that I was able to let go, in my mind, in many ways. After all, my two dear sons, Sean and Jason, were with me through all kinds of weather, and I could not imagine *not* being needed by them, and I certainly did not want them to be out of my life.

The three of us let go in the important ways, and now we are close by choice. We respect and honour one another in many ways all of the time. I am here for them, and they are there for me, just for the asking.

John and I celebrated our 25th anniversary on March 23, 2002. Sean officiated in our ceremony to renew our vows, and Jason gave a toast to me at the reception. Wow! If what they said to me, and about me, on that occasion is *letting go*, then I am all for it. I called us the "Three Musketeers" when we were alone in the world after my separation from their father, and that name suited us then, but not any longer. Now I have my husband sharing my life, but I know there are two other men in the world who love me totally with all my faults and all my virtues. They are still my greatest gifts to the world and that is a thought of which I will never let go.

LETTING GO

The time to go is drawing near,
The break is fast approaching.
To say goodbye's not been my style,
But, God, it will be cleansing.
Half my heart is sick with dread—
Half my heart is singing.
It seems that I have now grown up—
Why was it so long coming?
Along with me will come my Love—
My laughter, he'll be sharing.
I see the sun in the eastern sky—
For us, it is just rising.
For those to whom my body gave life—
My love is never ending.
But, goodbye, I say to my two sons—
Goodbye, now let's start living.

EULOGY TO MAX

Max was a cat owned by a friend named Eunice. He was a male through and through, and if he could have talked he would have had a very deep voice. When Eunice was away, I would walk over and feed Max and her female cat named Patches, and so I grew to care about them on an intimate level. I wrote this poem as a gift for Eunice when Max died.

Eunice was special to me because she was a woman who helped me find myself at a time when I was very lost. In 1988, when we finally sold our house at Cooking Lake and moved into the city, I took a course at Career College. Eunice was the instructor and she was wonderful. I will never forget one very significant event that occurred on the first day of classes.

This was my first venture out into the real world after my years of depression, and my self-esteem and self-worth were less than zero when added together. I was so nervous about being there, and about being expected to learn something, that I took Eunice aside and told her about my depression. Then I asked her if she thought that I was **teachable**. Do you realize how far down the intelligence scale one has to be in order to be considered **unteachable**? Anyway, I thought myself to be less intelligent than that! What a surprise to me when I came out with a 96% average, placing me at the top of the class! I was even asked to be a teacher's assistant for a few weeks, at which time I helped with marking of exam papers. So much for **unteachable**!

I do not remember how Eunice and I came to be friends after the class was finished, but we did and we enjoyed each other for as long as we were supposed to. I guess we did our work together, and then we just quietly drifted apart. I met her downtown, one day, when I was lunching with someone else and we chatted for a moment. We were happy to see one another, but neither made an attempt to rekindle the friendship. I am glad I found this poem because it has reminded me of a person who supported me through a time of transformation and growth. I shall never forget Eunice ... or that cat named Max.

EULOGY TO MAX

On four little legs he walked into your heart
And you knew right away this was Max.
He had such a way of making you laugh
And you loved how he made you relax.
Wee Max was a cat with character galore
All male, he liked to act tough.
His mate for life was a feline named Patches
To her, Sir Max was enough.
For so many years, Max was just like a child
Who took so much less than he gave.
He played and gave all each day of his life
And at the end, like a man, he was brave.
To Max, you gave a glorious gift—
You were there when his time came to die.
I'll bet that he felt no longer afraid
Because the love of his life was close by.
One day, when you walk through the tunnel of light
You will know you are safe when you see
Those four little legs on your dear little Max
Walking to you, dear Friend, with glee.

CLEANSED BY THE DIRT

This poem was inspired by an incident that happened in 1973. I was staying with some dear friends while I was going through the trauma of leaving my husband in Kelowna, and moving back to Edmonton with my two small sons. At that time, I did a lot of crying, and I did a lot of worrying, and I did a whole lot of talking about all of the things that scared me. One day, I returned to their home after being out and I was so sad and so low, that my chin felt like it was dragging on the floor. They were doing some landscaping at the time and the whole front yard was a mass of piles of dirt that needed to be spread.

My friend took one look at my long face and told me to come out to the yard. I did as I was told and he handed me a shovel and told me to get to work. I shovelled dirt for a longer time than I thought I was capable. When I was done, I was dirty and smelly and totally refreshed. I could not believe that physical labour could have such a powerful effect. I do not know, to this day, if this man was actually that wise, or if he was just tired of my whining and crying, and so figured that I would keep quiet if I was hauling dirt around. Whatever his motive was, I am grateful, because it helped me that day and showed me the power of physical work.

Usually I only expend energy emotionally and mentally, with very few physical interludes. It was great to know that when energy is expended physically, the other two areas get a much needed rest. That day I truly felt cleansed by the dirt.

To two special people
Thank you.
Wherever you are, I wish you peace.

CLEANSED BY THE DIRT

We, who live in the city, bathe
Or shower, at least, once a day.
We say that we feel so dirty,
So strive to wash impurities away.

The farmer who works in the soil
(A gift that God sent from above)
Is tired, but does not seem dirty
After performing his labour of love.

The stress that Man has created
Can make him unable to cope.
We bathe, and wash, and shower,
And put far too much faith in our soap.

When troubles appear too big in our lives
We should then to Nature revert.
The soil will wash all our sorrows away,
One might say we've been cleansed by the dirt.

UPON TURNING EIGHTEEN

This poem was another that was written upon request from my former *boss*, Reggie, for a friend of hers. I was surprised that I could write on demand for Reggie, whereas I could not do that for anyone else. I have kept this poem because it is a universal theme and because it is something I would have liked to have had when I turned eighteen. I have also kept it in my collection, because it reminds me that one person believed in my ability to write it.

My son often says that "a boy never gets respect in his own home town" and then cites Jesus as an example of the truth of these words. I take that even farther and say that one's talents are often taken for granted and not valued by one's own family. I was not encouraged to write by anyone in my home because it was something I always did, and so they did not feel that they needed to prod me on. They expected me to write because I had always done it. Unfortunately, I often read that as meaning the opposite, and thought that they did not believe in my abilities to put pen to paper.

So, Reggie was the first person to outwardly acknowledge my talents and gifts by encouraging me at every opportunity. I did all of her correspondence for her and was able to do that on her behalf by pretending to be *her* in my mind. I was so successful at it that I had to quit in 1995 because I had forgotten how to write from my own point of view. However, in those four years with her, I received feedback almost every day about my writing and was encouraged to do something with it. I took my time in deciding to believe her, but here I am, and her belief in my talents has now spread into many other areas. In fairness, upon asking my family for their opinions about creating a book, they all said they have wondered why it has taken me so long to get going. I guess they have always believed in me and I am shocked by how I misread their sentiments.

I will always be grateful to you, Reggie,
because you were my very dear friend, and
my very first fan.

UPON TURNING EIGHTEEN

Too soon the days of adulthood
Came knocking at your door!
Now we see a woman
Where a child once stood before.
Wasn't it only recently
That your mom stood and watched you play?
Where could all the years have gone
It just seems like yesterday.
So now you take the lessons
That your parents lovingly gave,
And apply them to your adult life
Knowing their strength will make you brave.
In the days as you grow older,
There will be times when you'll feel scared.
These are the times that you must remember
That they gave you life because they cared.
Sometimes you'll feel that adulthood
Is not all that you thought it would be.
There'll be times when you want to head for home
Back to the child who played in glee.
We each have a child within us
Who will keep us from growing old.
The child's our connection to the love of the world
And will fill our hearts with treasures untold.
So take your place now, dear one,
The world is waiting for you.
The future will be all that you make it—
There is nothing that <u>you</u> cannot do.

THE DREAM

In 1989, Sean and Janet drove to Ontario to visit her parents. One morning, a few days after they left, I was awakened very early by the phone and was surprised to hear Sean sounding so upset. Without any small talk, he immediately asked me if I was feeling alright. I said I was and he told me about the vivid dream that he had experienced just before waking that morning. He explained that it had been so real that he had to call because he was sure it had actually happened. He told me the details of the dream, and as soon as I hung up the phone, I sat down and penned this poem.

The house in the poem is the house at South Cooking Lake where he had spent ten years of his youth. It is also the house where we all experienced a lot of pain and learning; it was there that we lived when I was so sick with depression. This was not the happiest place in the world for Sean because I had given him the awesome responsibility of taking care of everything and everybody while I was indisposed for four years.

For all of their lives, I have told my sons that when I die I will never be too far away because I will speak to them through nature, such as through the songs of birds. This part was not in the dream, but I added it as something that I would have said to him in such a circumstance.

THE DREAM

He dreamed in sleep that his mother had died,
No warning, she was called from this earth.
He grieved at the loss of his original friend,
So close had they been since his birth.
To get by, henceforth, without her kind words
To him, left a hole in his life.
His mother knew well that he'd be alright
For he still had his wonderful wife.
One night as he sat in that house all alone,
And wondered how he'd ever cope
With all of the problems that life can present,
In pain, he felt drained of hope.
When all of a sudden he was not alone,
She sat there, like she'd never gone.
So calm, so peaceful, surrounded by Light,
They talked from dark until dawn.
From somewhere within him the questions came forth,
She guided response from his heart.
For all of the years he had been there for her,
This gift, and then she'd depart.
In peace, he sat there—fear suddenly gone!
He clung to the last words he heard,
"I always will be in touch with your heart,
Listen well to the song of each bird."

THE ANNIVERSARY

When Sean became engaged to Janet I thought my world would end, because I honestly believed that I needed him more than she did. That must sound rather strange for a mother to say, but it was true. Sean had taken care of me since he was four years old, and that is the sickest part of all. I let this child go through his whole childhood thinking that he was responsible for me, the supposed adult of the group. Through my years of going in and out of hospital with depression, he was the one who had to take care of our world while I was gone. John worked out of town and so the burden landed on Sean. He did a wonderful job, and I am lucky, to say the least, that I did not lose him along the way.

His impending marriage forced me to seek help from a therapist, who turned out to be a most blessed gift. This man helped me look into my soul to find the reasons why I clung to Sean so much. The findings were earth-shaking and through him, my real search to find myself began. Only through him could I take the girl out from behind the closed door. He came to Sean's wedding so that he could see the event that had caused me such anguish, and to give me some much-needed support. *God bless you, Dr. R.*

Sean and Janet have now been married for well over a decade and I am proud of them. I now know my place in his life and I have the distinction of being, in his eyes, his "#1 Fan" in the cheering section of his life. Thank you, Sean, for the sacrifices and the love you showed me when you should have been playing ball.

THE ANNIVERSARY

One year ago, I stood there
And watched him as he wed
The girl of his dreams, his sweetheart,
Soft words of love they said.
A magic filled the air all round
As I gave my son away,
So happy for them—so sad for me,
I remember the boy at play.
The rituals went on and on,
My heart begged them to stop,
But no one seemed to hear me;
One memory in every teardrop.
One year ago, I lived that day
And still I feel the pain
Of letting go of a piece of my life
That my heart had tried to retain.
A part of me feels pride and joy,
I see the love they feel has grown.
They show more kindness and caring
Than any couple that I've ever known.
So why do I feel such sadness
When I see their perfect blending?
For them, it was a beginning,
For me, it was an ending.

THE GRADUATE—1987

Sean seemed to be a constant source of inspiration to me in my poetry, and I think it was because he was the centre of so much that happened to me in those very difficult days. As I have said earlier, he took on the burden of caring for me at four years of age, and after that I let him have more responsibility than any child should ever carry. These poems cannot undo any of that, but they can show that I do honour him and his contributions to my growth.

Whenever Sean reached a milestone in his life such as Graduation, it struck me hard because each event brought me one step closer to having to live without him. As unhealthy as this may sound, it was a fact of my life at that time, and so I am telling it like it was.

I actually thought that I was going to die when Sean graduated in 1987 from Ardrossan High School. Fear of abandonment was huge in me, and since this child was a major care-giver in my life, his departure would have been devastating. Sad, but true!

A few days after the graduation banquet, I went into an exaggerated fear mode and said some things that rightfully upset Sean. He replied to me in a way that I deserved, but it sent me over the edge. I became suicidal and found myself in the psychiatric lockup ward that night. That was my last stay in hospital. After three weeks, I was told that I was not clinically depressed, but that I was one of the unhappiest women the doctor had ever met. That really blew me away—I could accept being *mentally ill*, but do not call me *unhappy*! The next day, I checked myself out and never returned. I decided that it was up to me to make some changes. It took a lot of work, a lot of time, and a lot of tears, but I am finally happy. I no longer rely on Sean (or anyone else) to get me through each day, but I love him and thank him for saving my life, in my eyes, so many times, so many years ago.

THE GRADUATE—1987

A heart bursts with pride.
The same heart is breaking.
A young man in cap and gown.
Looking proud.
Justifiably so.
Looking happy.
His whole life ahead of him.
The adventure excites him.
One corner of his heart is consumed in pain.
He knows why.
He looks through the mass of faces,
Searching for just one.
His eyes meet hers—both fill with tears.
With a half-smile and a nod,
She says to him,
"My son, I love you. I always have and
I always will. You are a man now and I must
set you free. I will miss you."
He knows what she has said,
Through his heart, not his ears.

For eighteen years, their hearts have been bound.
He nods back to her, his pride now larger than life.
His heart answers her back.
He knows that she will hear.
"I love you, Mom. You got me this far—
stay with me for the rest of the ride.
I will thank you, but you must know that
this is not Goodbye."
"This is just an intersection on the Road of
Life and I know which way I am going.
Remember, Mom, all roads lead home.
So smile, pretty lady, smile."
Quickly, he turns. His friends are waiting.
A chill goes through her—loneliness, again.
Just then, he turns toward her and makes a funny face.
She laughs in spite of herself.
She takes a deep breath.
In that one second, her pain has begun to ease.
Her little boy is alive and seemingly quite well,
And living in the heart of THE GRADUATE.

THE ROSE

Life is like a dew-drenched rose,
Hanging on a vine.
I look at it and crave it,
And yearn to make it mine.
Its beauty, it unnerves me,
So unworthy do I feel.
Its fragrance so enticing,
My heart begins to reel.
And so I stand and look in awe,
Trying to reason why
I would deserve to pluck it,
"No," I say, "Not I."
And as I stand deciding
Should I or should I not;
She quickly reaches and picks my rose
Apparently with no thought.
I've lost the rose, but what about life?
Is it, too, passing me by?
Too much thought, and too little risk,
And too little faith have I.
I am letting them get the roses;
For what purpose was I born?
I am afraid if I grab for the flower,
In my haste, I'll be cut by a thorn.

PEARLS AND LACE

This poem is about my daughter-in-law, Janet, on her Graduation day. She wore a pink dress that was covered with a fine lace. At that time, I was selling Avon in a big way and a new perfume had come out called *Pearls and Lace*. I gave her a bottle with all of the lotions that went with it and put it in a basket that was lined with lace. I laid a string of pearls across it. She loved it and so that became her perfume of choice at that time. It also seemed fitting to be the title of the poem about her.

I was so happy and grateful that she chose to love Sean. He was such a great kid, but he was so shy, and he had never had a girlfriend before Janet. I wanted him to be happy, but I did not want to lose him. However, she made it very clear that she valued me in her life as well; I needed that, and we became good friends.

I knew the first time I set eyes on her that they would marry one day because they looked like brother and sister … in some other life, they probably were. I thank Janet for being a good wife to my dear son. Not many girls would have measured up in my eyes, but I was right then and she is still right for him now. Their life has been full of challenges, and I know it did not quite follow the path that she thought it would, but still she sticks by him knowing she is part of the Plan.

PEARLS AND LACE

Pearls and lace on a gown of pink,
Adorn our princess on her night of nights.
The stars in her eyes,
Outshine the stars in the sky.
She is happy. She is lovely. She is loved.

The man on her arm,
Is the man in her heart.
He sees more than her gown of pink.
To him, her beauty is a light
That shines from somewhere deep within.

The pearls and lace give life to her gown.
Her smiling eyes lighten up her face.
This lovely young woman,
And this handsome young man
Are the Prince and Princess of Fate.

Pearls and lace on a gown of pink,
Remind her of that night, so rare.
Not strife, not war,
Not age, not death
Will take the stardust from her hair.
It landed there as he gazed at her,
And she smiled her love to him.

MY HUSBAND

I will be talking about my husband, John, in connection with other poems, but I just want to acknowledge the wonderful influence that he has had on my life. John taught me about the importance of being true to myself, and thus, to our relationship. I taught him about the importance of being true to himself, and thus, to our relationship. We are as different as night and day, while at the very same time, being so connected that it is hard to tell where one of us ends and the other begins. We are both better people for being married to one another.

I wish to make note here of the piles of money that John has willingly expended on me in my search to find my heart's passion. You may think I am overstating the fact, but believe me, I am not! He has never once complained, and has never once said that he had reached the end of his financial rope with me. John is my best friend, my bonus from God, and my *VP in Charge of Finance*. He taught me to laugh, and he taught me how to find a little lightness in very serious issues. I have not succeeded in doing that all the way, but I am a million miles past where I was when I began this trek. Once again, I am not exaggerating!

Thank you, John, for loving me so well. You started out being my greatest lesson, and now you are my highest reward. No matter how long we have together on this earth, I will love you forever. You are my best angel!

MY HUSBAND

A simple man, yet complex.
A humble man, yet proud.
A stubborn man, yet yielding.
A giving man, yet always holding back.
Sometimes, not often,
I get to see the little boy who romped the hills of Wales.
I see the tender, vulnerable heart
That his mother knew and loved.
But, mostly, I see the man,
The hard worker, the provider.
I see weariness.
I see frustration.
I see dreams unrealized.
I also see strength unlike any other.
I see loyalty unfamiliar to most.
I see depth that would challenge any ocean.
I see love wrapped like a secret present.
This man, my husband, is my connection to the earth.
No matter how high I fly,
I am safe—
He is waiting on the ground, feet firmly planted.
My man wants to give me so much—
He wants to give me the world.
My man is a silly man—
All I ever really wanted was HIM.

HE BUILT ME A HOUSE

John told me that he did not know how else to show me he loved me, so he would build me a house. He must have loved me a lot because it was the biggest house I had ever seen—a 4000 square foot bungalow not including the utility room and garage. It was so long that it looked like a motel. We had no money when we started to build, so in order to get a loan without any collateral, we borrowed the small sum of $2000, bought all the lumber we could, and then paid it back as quickly as possible. We did that a number of times until we had enough of the house built to qualify for a mortgage. It took two years of perseverance and never-ending work to get this humble home built. When John was not working, he was at the lake building the house, so unless I worked right along beside him, we did not see much of each other.

I have never seen such spirit, such persistence, such dedication and such love as I saw in John during that time. In some ways, I was sorry to see the building phase come to an end because it had been a time of togetherness for us. On November 25, 1978, we moved into our dream house - or at least that is what we thought it was!

We had many happy times, but something was very wrong there. I got so sick with depression, and Jason, my younger son, was severely plagued with Obsessive Compulsive Disorder. John was away most of the time and, in some ways, it felt like he had built me a house, and then left me there out in the country where I did not want to be at all. The fear of being alone set in and I did not think that I would ever make it out of that house alive. A shaman suggested that because we had cut down **all** of the trees, we had actually brought a curse upon ourselves from the gods of nature. That belief system is not my reality, but looking at the results, it felt like it could be true. The Native beliefs have held up for a long time, so who am I to argue? Something was dreadfully wrong there, and our lives only improved when we left that house and moved back to the city. Most people find peace in country living—I thought I had gone to Hell.

HE BUILT ME A HOUSE

He built me a house, a castle of sorts,
A gift from a king to his queen.
He said it was a way to show me his love,
Then made reality out of a dream.
For two long years, he battled fatigue
And changed lumber and nails into life,
An artist at work keeping beat with the words,
"I must build a home for my wife."
I remember a day—the heat was so thick,
I watched him nail rafters above.
The sweat was pouring from off of his brow,
A visible sign of his love.
I had never before seen such love at work,
He toiled from morning 'til night.
One day he declared that his work was all done,
I cried at the beautiful sight.
In myths of old the tale would end there—
"And they all lived happily after."
I'm sad to say that this is no tale,
Soon tears would still all the laughter.

OUR TENTH ANNIVERSARY

In March of 2002, John and I celebrated our 25th wedding anniversary, by throwing a huge party and dance because we deserved every celebratory moment of it. We felt confident that we had accepted all the challenges, and passed all the tests that we had been given, thus far, as a couple, and as individuals. When this poem was written, in March of 1987, there was much pain in our everyday lives due to the nervous breakdown that put me out of commission for four years. At the time of writing, I had yet to go through one last three-week stint in hospital (when I was admitted because I was suicidal). Looking back at that scene, and knowing what I know now, this poem takes on a different tone for me.

In 1987, I said that the laughter was returning, and perhaps in comparison to the sadness and depression, it must have seemed that way at the time. However, as strange as it may sound, I do not remember being happy again until at least 1992 when John had a heart attack and emergency bypass surgery. That is when we addressed our own mortality as individual persons, and as a couple. We realized that our marriage was a living, breathing entity that needed to be cared for, not just once in a while, but every minute of every day in some capacity or another.

Essentially, we were given a wake-up call, and wake up we did! From that day on, we started to consciously work on all the little unfinished issues in every aspect of our lives. I am amazed that we survived all that we did, but I am even prouder of the effort that we both exerted to make us a better duo than we had ever thought we could be. We are an amazing couple, and I *will* say so myself!

Marilyn Avient

OUR TENTH ANNIVERSARY

Ten years, together for richer, for poorer.
Mostly poorer,
Trying to get ahead.
Trying! Trying! Trying!
Ten years, sometimes bliss, sometimes misery.
Then joy, as love is reconfirmed.
Suffering with one another,
As personal grief comes our way.
Still caring. Still loving. Still laughing.
Ten years, together only sometimes.
True to each other,
Our love is greater than our need for others.
Our love stronger than most,
For we survive.
I wait. You come home. I am happy.
Ten years, in sickness and in health.
Three years of hell for me.
Three years of hell for you.
Too sick to see you suffering.
Too prideful for you to tell me.
The laughter is silenced.
Helplessness can be heard from every corner.
You cannot fix me so just hold my hand.
Your touch has healing powers.
Smile at me ... I crave it!

Ten years, and we face another ten.
Can we make it?
Our love is strong enough.
The laughter is returning.
Shall we face the same direction?
Shall we look to the sunrise?
The sunset is time gone by.
The sunrise holds promises.
Let's hold hands and smile, have faith,
And communicate from our hearts.
I know we can make it. I know it.

March 1987

FINALLY TO MY DAD

The anger is behind me.
The words have all been said.
I wish that you could hold me,
But no ... you still are dead.

I loved you, then I hated you
With all my heart and soul.
You went away, I waited ...
Many years, I was not whole.

Now I am well; I see you smile.
Time now to say, "Forgive."
On pleasant thoughts I'll spend awhile,
In peace, I yearn to live.

You and Mom, to me gave life,
I know you did your best.
The anger and the pain are gone,
I love you ... now you rest.

THE BALLOON PEDDLER

When I found this poem, I was amazed at how true the ideas expressed here had become—even more so now than at the time when it was written in 1991. I read it to my husband, John, who is my balloon peddler, and even he was amazed at the truths told here.

I have always been the dreamer and the one whose head and heart are in the clouds in ways that often preclude real life. Although I still float away once in a while, I feel that my escapades into the clouds are more tangible, and more structured because I am more consciously spiritual now than I was in the early 1990's. It was all a process that began with whimsical dreams that evolved into thoughts that, only lately, have taken on any semblance of reality. Now I am seeing how absolutely beautiful those dreams were!

The only line that I would change in 2002 would be the last one. As we become older, my husband and I know that one day one of us will be left alone due to the passing of the other. If I am the one who is left, I will not die from grieving. I will be enveloped in sadness for a very long time, but I will recover. I will get back on my feet, and somehow I will find a way to let myself soar above the clouds once more. Perhaps that will be the most grounding event of my life, and I will have to decide at that time to find all of my magic right here on Earth, just the way my balloon peddler used to do. On the other hand, it may be the event that will show me that I can fly on my own, and just his memory will be enough to keep me safe and grounded.

THE BALLOON PEDDLER

He is the peddler; I am the balloons.
Day in and day out I float above him—
happy, contented and never quite touching the ground.
No need—he is my connection.
A gentle breeze catches my fancy
And suddenly I have wings, I know I can fly.
He stretches patiently, lovingly.
Slowly, the breeze is strangled by heavy, humid heat.
I deflate. He knew I would. He is ready.
He restores me so I can fly again.
Without warning, a strong, urgent wind takes hold of me.
I am out of control. I rise higher, higher, higher.
I reach for the sun—fighting him, begging him to let me go.
His feet rise off the ground as he tries to keep up.
Knowing. Determined.
He hangs on as long as he needs to.
No wind blows forever. In its exhaustion, I crash!
He catches me.
The experience has taken much out of me.
But I am safe now. He relaxes. I rest. I am renewed.
Soon, I am floating once more, merrily ... knowing he is
there, his feet firmly planted on the ground.
IF...one morning he is not there ...
I shall quietly drift away ... never to be seen again.

LOST

A little mouse ran away from home
To the lake, so frozen white.
The horizon disappeared before his wee eyes;
Back, forward, left and right.

Panic gripped his tiny heart,
"Where am I going? Where am I from?"
A mountain ahead where a wave did freeze,
"Impossible," he thought, "to overcome."

Stealthily surveying the white terrain
Footprints behind him lay.
"Now that I've left my mark on the world,
Help me!" the mouse did pray.

"Should I go forward or should I go back?
No one knows the adventure I'm on."
The last light of day was leaving the sky—
Would the tiny mouse last 'til dawn?

He laid his tired body down
Wearily wishing to die.
He thought of home, so safe and warm,
That black hole where he liked to hide.

"Why did I leave that hole so safe?
Did I really think I could follow a dream?
No one cares about a tiny mouse
'Less I scare them and make them scream!"

"I have a choice that I can make;
Stop; go forward; go back.
I have no talents to offer the world
Or is it the courage I lack?"

Slowly, the wee mouse started to rise,
As though with decision resolved.
"I'm known only for being afraid.
For that sin I'll be absolved."

"Dying's too easy; home is no more,
So onward, one step at a time.
If one of those steps should be my last;
At least quitting will not be my crime."

Step by step, over miles of white,
To his life, that brave mouse did cling.
Under cloudy skies, I heard him cry.
In sunshine, I heard him sing.

UNCONDITIONAL LOVE

Strangely enough, here is another take on the scenario about a balloon peddler. In this scenario, I am the peddler and my children are the balloons. After all these years, I smile at the fact that on one day I see myself as being the one who needs to be taken care of, and on another I envision myself as being in charge. Perhaps this is evidence of the duality and the versatility that we humans possess.

In this particular selection, I am struggling with letting my children go, so that they can fly on their own. If I had had my way many years ago, that would never have happened, but luckily for all of us, the boys knew that they needed to fly away, and so they did. I realize that that is in keeping with each of our life-plans, because I wanted to have my own freedom, and they certainly needed theirs. I am content to get on with my life, knowing that they are flying with ease on their own. No matter my role—the balloons or the peddler—I have been given many lessons to learn, and, for the most part, I have been a good student!

As philosophical as I may sound about letting my boys fly away, the truth is that I fought the process every step of the way. I honestly thought that I would die when my boys ceased to need me on a daily basis. Accepting the inevitable was one of the hardest things I had to do, but when the time came, I did it valiantly. I am proud of what I had to conquer in order to get from there to here, and as a bonus, my sons are proud of me as well.

UNCONDITIONAL LOVE

He stood there on the corner
At morning, noon, and night.
To everyone who passed that way,
The balloon peddler; a common sight.

"Balloons!" he called out, loud and clear,
"Balloons, I have for you.
Any colour under the sun—
Red, yellow, purple, or blue."

His arm never seemed to tire
Of holding the balloons so high.
The balloons danced proud in the summer breeze
And wished that they could fly.

No matter what else he had to do
The balloons, he never let go.
He treated them all like children
Who needed his love to grow.

A raging storm caught him by surprise
And tried to take them away.
He fought the wind; he fought the balloons
Who did not seem to want to stay.

As soon as the storm was over,
He said, "It's time to set you free,
You seem to want to fly on your own,
Now go see what you want to see."

And now he sits on the corner
With eyes turned up to the sky.
They know that he will be waiting
For one glimpse as his loved ones fly by.

I WONDER…

I wonder how my dad felt
As he wrote his "Thought for the Day."
Did he ever feel discouraged?
Did he say all he wanted to say?

Did he ever hold a thought back
In case someone else would see?
Did he ever want to write a phrase
That lacked human dignity?

I know that he is watching
Each word that my hand writes.
I wish that he would write through me
As I sit here in the night.

I wonder if he shakes his head
Or raises one eyebrow
When I dare to write of death and gloom
Or other things he'd never allow.

But no, I think he is smiling
And saying, "It's alright,
Better to feel and write it,
Then let it go out into the night."

THE SIBLINGS

This poem is painful for me. I created a role for myself as a child and I continued to play this role well into my adult years. My role of self-appointed peacemaker in our house came from the fact that I would feel physically ill in the presence of any disharmony.

As an adult, I held all the family gatherings, but knew that something was amiss when I began to suffer violent abdominal pain at every family encounter. I realized one day that perhaps I was trying to pull people together against their will, and the pain was merely an indicator that I was using sand-bags against a tidal wave.

One attempt I made to bind us all together came in the form of a family history book, which I researched, compiled, wrote, and edited during an entire year of my life. Mom financed this book and gave it to all the members of the family for Christmas that year. I thought by being in the same book, we would all become magically close. I was disappointed in the response, but some good did come of it because Mom was happy knowing that we would all know our histories, and she did not need to worry about that anymore.

2007—Mom passed away in 2005 and before she died she told me that her greatest fear was that the four of us would lose touch with one another.

In Sept 2006, Sharon, Barbara, David and I had a 10 day reunion; it was wonderful and I know that Mom is happy that we finally all connected. Thankfully, in essence, we changed the last lines of the poem to a much happier version. Now, I truly am a sister!

THE SIBLINGS

You are my brother and sisters—
I wish we were closer friends.
Matching blood flows in our veins,
Does there, our likeness end?

As helpless tots, we shared a meal,
Over toys, we bitterly fought.
We had the same rules to follow,
What we could do and what we could not.

At Christmas time, we gave our gifts,
On birthdays, we shared a cake.
Easter brought out our Sunday best,
Summers, we camped by the lake.

We loved the same mother and father,
In them, we shared a bond.
They gave to us all that they had;
The love they shared was strong.

Then the inevitable happened,
We grew up and we grew away.
Dad passed away in springtime,
Before the flowers bloomed in May.

Many years have passed since then,
Each of us close to our mother.
I wished for more with my sisters,
But have spent more time with my brother.

Sadness fills me as I realize
The fantasy I have made.
As adults, we aren't a close family;
As children, we should have stayed.

We all have roles in the drama,
Each playing our separate parts.
How could we share so many things,
But forget to share our hearts?

Marilyn Avient

THANK GOD ...

Thank God I'm alive,
I've known much pain,
But today I am claiming as mine.
Outside of my realm
I see clouds, I feel rain,
Inside, I am sunny and fine.
From where comes the light
That shines out of my eyes,
And makes me feel cozy and warm?
It comes from my soul
Who knows no disguise
And who daily keeps me from harm.

A KIND AND GENTLE LADY

This poem is about my mother. She is a woman who has spent her life trying to better the life she had as a child. I know she decided very early on in life that one day, her family would never suffer the way she did. They would have a clean house, a quiet family life, and clean clothes. There would be no drinking, and there would be plenty of food to eat at every meal. She succeeded in this quest without one omission. As I told her one day when we had a very serious talk, the only thing that I could fault her on was that with all the hard work she did, there was no time for little girls. I was a lonely child and my childhood memories of my mother revolve around the noise of her working in the kitchen—pots and pans being moved around, bread being kneaded, water running, liquids boiling on the stove and her busy feet rushing around trying to keep up with the demands of her mind.

I grew up feeling the pain that she lived with, but about which she never spoke. When I finally did hear some of the not-so-pleasant details, I felt as if I were hearing them for the second time because, on an inner level, I had known them all along. Because I was so sensitive, Mom lived the pain, and I felt it. Pain needs no details, it just is.

My mother and I have had more clashes than she and any of my siblings have had. She has pushed spiritual and emotional buttons for me that no one else has done. The wonderful thing is that we have talked about all of this, and I finally admitted to her that I have spent my whole life trying to get her approval. We have spoken of things that many people never bother to talk about, and now I feel like we have finally landed in a place of peace.

I miss you, Mom.

A KIND AND GENTLE LADY

A kind and gentle lady
Has been in my life for so long.
So plagued by doubt and racked with pain,
For us, she tried to be strong.
The doubt is whether she deserved to be loved,
The pain—from ages past.
So long she has suffered she thinks it is she;
While still a child, her die had been cast.
She did everything a mother can do
To give her children what she never had.
From early dawn to darkest night
She slaved, but still she felt sad.
It merely was a common sight
To see this gentle lady cry.
Despair was spilling from out of her soul,
But nobody questioned why.

If I could have one wish in this life,
I would wish her one day of peace,
To let her feel the love that is hers,
I would wish that her pain would cease.
A word to this gentle lady from me,
"You didn't deserve the pain.
The little girl that was, still is—
just love her and she'll live again."
"You think that you are too old to change,
when you're too old to change, you are dead.
If you embrace the child within you
she will make sense of the life you have led."
This kind and gentle lady
Who has been in my life all along
Gave me life and for that, I thank her,
From her I learned to be strong.

Marilyn Avient

LESSONS AS BLESSINGS

Blessings fall around me;
They could be compared to snow.
Some of them are lessons
Designed to help me grow.

Family, friends, and self-esteem
Are perceived now through new eyes.
I have no need for illness
Or the refuge of disguise.

For every hurt that comes my way
There's a lesson to be learned.
Pain used to be my enemy;
Into friendship now it has turned.

No creature placed upon this earth
Is done so carelessly.
My spirit has a task for me
I keep searching endlessly.

I know that I choose the ones
Who will help me reach my goal.
My body is the worker,
Management comes from my soul.

I will never stop searching for truth
Until my work on earth is done.
I will never stop fighting the fight,
Until I know that I have won.

TWO PUPPIES

Cleo and Clancey were two lovable members of our family for ten years. Cleo was the canine version of me in that she was scared of her own shadow, she was a people pleaser, and she was only strong when in service to others. I know that she was a dog who would have dragged me out of a burning house, or if that was not possible, she would have lain there with me to take care of me as we burned together. Not a pretty picture, but I know she loved me enough to do that. Others saw her as skittish and nervous, and a little stupid, but I did not. Some kitchen cabinet workers were at our house very soon after I got her. She stood between me and them and growled continuously to let them know that she would not tolerate them coming any closer. I felt very safe in her presence.

Clancey was the opposite. He was lovable to everyone and yet appeared to need no one. He went through two hip surgeries in a period of two years, and what a brave little trooper he was. The vet said that he was the ideal patient because even in his pain, his sweet, gentle nature prevailed. He was a searcher of freedom and took every opportunity to explore the world. One time when my mother was staying at our house, she took him for a walk in the field and he got away. She soon gave chase, and he would let her get just within reaching distance, and then take off again. Mom got her exercise that day, and Clancey had a wonderful romp in the open field.

I had them put to sleep—I killed them—on June 27, 1988. I cannot go into the details even yet, but from the moment that it was obvious they were dead, I felt physically ill at what I had done. I had good practical reasons for doing what I did because we were moving to town, but that did not help my feelings of guilt. Finally, with the dawning of the new millennium, I felt it was time to give my love once again to two more dogs. Many times, I have mistakenly called them "Cleo" and "Clancey" and I have wondered if, on some level, I recognize that the same two beautiful souls are with me once more.

TWO PUPPIES

To Cleo and Clancey with love!

When I die, I know I will see two puppies running up to me.
One is black; one is white;
One is tall; one is slight.
When puppies die, they go to Heaven,
Of that, you can be sure.
I know God loves the meek and mild
and those whose souls are pure.
Cleo, my black darling, had a heart of pure sunshine.
Lived to be loved and that she was
For years numbering more than nine.
She thought she was a "people"
When on the couch she sat.
She would lie in the darkened hallway,
I would trip and call her "brat."
Some people thought her a coward,
so nervous she seemed to be,
But I felt safe when she was there
I knew she'd take care of me.
Clancey, on the other hand
Was as white as the driven snow,
Until the door would open
Then into the mud, he would go.
To me, he was an Irish rogue,
Lively and loved to be free.
Always watching for an open gate
Like the world he wanted to see.

Clancey had three loves in life—Cleo, us, and food.
Even with a cast upon his leg
No change in his constant good mood.
These puppies each had a place in our lives
That will not be filled again.
We gave to them; they gave to us—
They died, and I chose when.
Someday, I will forgive myself for decisions made that day.
My only comfort is that when I die
They will greet me and we'll play.
I picture them in a great big yard
No storms and no closed gates.
Clancey has a bowl of food.
Cleo just sits and waits.

Marilyn Avient

THE LONE GOLFER

I turned my head to the hole before
The rattle of clubs bouncing in a bag,
Nonchalant and oblivious of my eyes upon him
He strolled along the fairway to the green
Hopefully....The Lone Golfer.

He came upon us and we let him pass.
So young, so carefree, undaunted,
He swung the swing that only youth can know.
We watched wordlessly, waiting
As he sauntered on....The Lone Golfer.

I watched him move between grass and trees,
Now on the fairway, now in the rough.
His pace never changed, he never did smile.
He walked out of my view, out of my life
Into his future ... The Lone Golfer.

THE OLD MAN

The day we buried my father was a day that could only be described as surreal. That is a common reaction when a loved one dies, and so I think that I had to find something that was real to attach to the memory. To do this, I picked an old man standing on Whyte Avenue in Edmonton, Alberta on April 18, 1977.

In 2002, even funerals have changed. No more do you see the snake-like chain of vehicles slowly following funeral cars that are carrying the casket of the deceased and the grieving family members. Traffic lights did not have to be heeded by such a procession; traffic would stop in all directions until the last car went by. People used to stop what they were doing and, in their silence, show respect for the neighbours who had lost a loved one. I remember funeral processions going down our street as a child, and everyone and everything being so quiet that you could literally hear a pin drop. Oh, how I miss those once time-honoured traditions.

By 1977, less respect for funerals had already begun. That is why this one old man stood out for me. I remember thinking when I saw him, "Dad would like that, because he would have done the same." I thanked the man with my heart that day, and then later decided to honour him with this poem. I know that he is dead now, because he was very old then, and I truly hope that someone paid homage to him as he passed by on his final trip down the streets of our city.

Some traditions did not need to be put aside with the electronic age and this was one of them. I have this picture in my mind of people hurrying to a funeral, then speeding down the shortest route to the cemetery (if they go), and then sending a sympathy card by e-mail. This saddens me, and I am glad that I have one old man to remind me of the days when people took the time to honour one another in this way.

Rest in peace, dear gentle man, and thank you.

THE OLD MAN

April, a sunny day, crowded streets.
Lunch hour is over. Workers hurry. For them, an ordinary day.
A snake with all its eyes lit up follows as though mesmerized,
Two black, shiny cars. Slowly moving,
Purposefully moving; block by miserable block.
One black car full of people. Sad people,
Blank and staring people. Looking, but not seeing.
For them, no street exists.
Second black car. One long oak box. A loved one.
Some heart is breaking. Could be your relative.
Could be mine. Could be you. Could be me.
On a street corner, same as the rest; an old man stands.
Looking, waiting.
As the oak box passes, his hat comes off,
His hand goes to his heart. He bows his head.
His quiet act of homage stands out loudly.
Noisy workers are quiet in comparison.
This old man had lived long; had felt Death; knew the pain.
He respected Death for soon it would be his.
Only one girl in the long black car saw the old man.
Her only remembrance of that special day
When slowly they drove to fill her father's freshly dug grave.

Ten years have passed since that day,
And only the memory of a man on the corner, paying respects,
Makes her really believe that her dad is dead.
Just one old man, hand to heart, brings pain.
But now, at least, she waits no more.

THE VISITATION

As is often the case with severe depression, suicide was a constant possibility for me. My father had died in 1977 and I missed him dreadfully. I always said that I would give anything to be with him, no matter the cost. One night I had just gone to bed and closed my eyes when the vision began. I was standing on a hill and in the valley I saw a throng of thousands. I could see my father in the very middle wearing a maroon coloured shirt, which I can still perceive in my mind as being warm and cosy. Instinctively, I knew that all the people in the crowd were dead. Dad waved at me and I waved back. I awoke immediately and marvelled at what I had just seen.

Two nights later it happened again, and again I saw Dad and I again I turned him down when he beckoned me to go with him. Again, he had on the maroon shirt.

The next day I called my mom to ask about the shirt. She said that she had bought that shirt for Dad about six months before he died, and he had worn it every day until he went into hospital where he died. She said that he had loved it because it was the softest and cosiest shirt that he owned and he valued its warmth in his weakened condition. I had not seen him at home in those six months so I had never seen the shirt, but it was verification for me that my Dad really did send this message to me.

THE VISITATION

I saw my Dad amidst a crowd,
He turned and he saw me.
He beckoned me to follow him—
I pretended not to see.

The crowd, it had no faces
As though all alone he stood.
Forced myself back to consciousness,
My heart, it felt like wood.

Not many nights passed by me
'Til the same crowd passed my view.
Again, same face I recognized,
He looked up as though on cue.

This time he stepped out of the crowd,
He motioned me with his hand,
"Come, my Judy, follow me!"
I turned away at his command.

I awoke and I was crying,
Non-belief at what I had done.
Given the chance, I thought I would follow him
Like the moon daily follows the sun.

That dream, it was a message,
Only now I see it so clear.
For years, I have felt so guilty,
But I could not shed a tear.

What my Dad was offering me
Is not easy to explain.
If I had agreed to follow him
Today, I would feel no pain.

He let me know that I had a choice
To die or else to live.
If such an offer could be refused
There must be more that I have to give.

ACCEPTANCE

Easy to accept the presents
Underneath the Christmas tree.
Easy to accept a letter
That was written just for me.

Easy to accept the praises
When I have done something good.
Easy to accept the compliment
When looking better than I normally would.

Hard to accept the critic
When I am not up to par.
Hard to accept the failure
When not successful as you are.

Hard to accept reality
That death is the final test.
Hard to accept the brutal truth—
I never will be best!

A LOVE STORY

This appears to be fictional, but I believe it to be a story of my lifetime immediately before this one. I have no tangible proof that this is so, but my heart tells me it is. I have always had an emotional attachment to England even though I have never lived there in this lifetime. I used to sit and cry and wish to 'go home'. One time the feeling was so strong that John agreed to let me make a trip to Britain alone. I did not go, and so I will never know what would have happened.

I have always felt my name should be Sara. One time when John came home and woke me up from a sound sleep, I asked him if "Richard" was home yet. He asked "Who?" and I said, "Richard" in a most frustrated tone as though he should know who that was. I remember getting up from that nap and being very sad (sadder than usual) for days afterwards.

I have seen the scene of Sara meeting Richard at the train many times in my mind, and to this day, it is as real as any other memory of this lifetime. I was born after the war, and yet I knew all the war songs as a child, and can cry over many of them even now. My parents did not own any recordings of these songs, and so it was unusual for a child my age to know them so intimately. Also, since I was born in Canada three years after World War II had ended, it is strange that, as a young child, I would hold my ears at night to keep from hearing the war planes flying overhead. That is a sound that I can hear in my mind to this day.

I do not believe that there is any such thing as fiction. I think it is truth that is remembered on a soul level, and we know it, but we do not know how we know it. This story comes from my soul, but I will not mind if you receive it as fiction.

A LOVE STORY

Sara, with the laughing eyes,
Sara, kind of heart.
Her soldier's name was Richard,
Too soon, they had to part.
In war, these two were lovers,
They each were the other's best friend.
Those hours they spent together
Were too beautiful to end.
They dreamed of peace tomorrow
With no buzz of planes overhead,
No blackened window curtains,
No lists of soldiers dead.
Together they danced in canteens
Pretending to be so brave.
Dreading the coming moment
When goodbye they would have to wave.
Day after day she would sit and wait
Her ear to the gramophone.
"Auf Wiederseh'n" and "Now is the Hour";
Sara cried as the lyrics droned on.

Outside the world raged on in fight,
All life seemed coloured black.
Sara kept the hope alive
That her soldier soon would be back.
Just once her prayers were answered
She stood waiting out in the rain.
For a few short hours together
He travelled many more by train.
Richard bravely fought the foe
But it was Sara who passed away
God needed her soul for another
"Loved," her epitaph did say.
With no time for forgetting
Sara again was earthly bound -
She saw her new daddy—a soldier,
"I'm safe—my Richard I've found!"

TIME FOR CHANGE

What fear? I know that I can handle
Anything that comes my way.
Mother Earth just keeps on turning
Paying no heed to what I say.

If only I could stop my heart
From jumping out of my chest.
If only I could persuade myself
What happens is all for the best.

Worrying is non-productive ...
I know that in my heart!
Perhaps my heart should tell my mind,
But old habits are slow to part.

Trying, oh, how I'm trying
To change my former ways.
Fearing, worrying, fretting
Have darkened more than too many days.

I must defeat this enemy,
Too cowardly to show his face.
Too long I let him lead the way
Now it's my turn to set the pace.

THE FLOUR QUEEN

This is a fun poem that put into words the teasing my family always gave me about my messy baking habits. Oh, how could one little girl make so much mess? The funny part is that when I am in the midst of the baking, I do not have any concerns about the chaos I am creating. I just throw all caution to the wind and dive in, and that is how I look when I am done—like I have jumped head first into a bale of flour!

When John built our big house at Cooking Lake, he intentionally created a huge kitchen for me. I believe his words were, "Not even you could mess up a kitchen this size!" Well, he came home one day when I was doing some Christmas baking, and he had to eat his words, because I had managed to spread baking pans and utensils from one end of the thirty foot room to the other. And it took weeks to clean up all of the flour that had been flying!

We have laughed a lot about this and so it is preserved in a poem. I do not bake anymore, so this talent of mine would have been lost in the archives of time, but for this writing. But let me add this—the mess was all worthwhile because, when I did bake, I was one heck of a success, and I know that they will all vouch for that!

THE FLOUR QUEEN

Christmas music is playing,
Delightful aroma fills the air.
The cookies are in the oven
There's flour everywhere.
It's become a family pastime
To sit and watch me bake.
No matter how easy the recipe,
A catastrophic mess I make.
I always tell my husband,
"I can't be cute, and efficient too!"
"You're right about that, Honey,
You've got flour all over you."
Sometimes I envy those women
Who can clean and wipe as they go.
I start with good intentions,
What happens, I'll never know.
In everything I do in life
I'm careful not to slip,
But in my culinary adventures,
I jump in and 'let her rip'.
Thank God for this one place in life
Where I can make a mess
Without prior thought of approval
Nor waiting for a caress.

HAPPINESS—WHERE ARE YOU?

Poetry was one of my most valued healing tools. I loved the way I felt after I successfully put a poem onto paper. In fact, that feeling was my first experience with inner peace and happiness. As I healed from my years of depression, I clamoured towards anything that felt even remotely like satisfaction or success. This was my last official poem of that era, and it was written in 1992.

On the day I wrote it, I was standing at the kitchen sink peeling carrots when I heard a voice in my head say, "Go write a poem." I said, "I don't want to write a poem. I want to peel carrots." The voice repeated its message and I looked at the table, where a paper and pencil were laying in readiness. I did not remember placing them there, so I thought I had better do what I was told.

I sat down without any idea of what I could or should write. Silly me, I did not need to know—my hand started flying across the paper! Within ten minutes, and without any apparent work on my part, this poem was there, word for word, as it appears today. I accepted this poem as a congratulatory gift straight from God and I am happy to share it with you.

HAPPINESS—WHERE ARE YOU?

I used to wonder where happiness was—
I searched and searched in vain.
I scanned the faces and eyes that I loved
And explored the surrounding terrain.
No luck had I—it's all a myth,
No happiness to be found.
I went inside to search my soul,
Not knowing just where I was bound.
The walls were lined with cobwebs
And reeked the stench of neglect.
No wisp of air; no sign of love;
No life could I detect.
or years, I sat in darkness,
I floundered and gasped for air.
I waited for someone to find me.
I waited for someone to care.
So tired of waiting for rescue,
I started relieving each shelf
Of the cobwebs, dust, and garbage
That I had gathered and heaped on myself.
The cobwebs were sticky and wanted to stay,
The dust was thick and black.
The garbage was heavy and painful to move—
No matter, I made my attack.

I cleaned until I thought I would drop,
Some told me to let the dust lie.
I knew that I must keep working
Or I would choke on the dust and die.
With power anew, I continued to clean
The corners and shelves of my soul,
To uncover the me, that was, and could be
Had become my ultimate goal.
One day I saw a sparkle and shine
Where dust had formerly laid.
I wept glad tears for my triumph
And rejoiced in the progress I'd made.
My eyes, by then, were used to the dark,
So long had I been without light.
While toiling I discovered a window
That opened to a glorious sight.
I saw a glowing, glittering world
So alive with wonders to see.
My eyes were able to focus
From light that was shining from me.
I used to wonder where happiness was—
I searched and searched in vain.
I found it living within me
And hiding under cobwebs and pain.

AND NOW THE DOOR IS OPEN ...

Finally
I feel the fresh air blowing on my face
and I am invigorated and liberated at last.
I thought that I had been held prisoner
and that no one wanted me out in the world amongst them
—at least not as my *real* self.
I thought I had to be the way
I perceived them wanting me to be
and, of course, that is a fallacy.
I know now that I needed to be *there* in order to *get here.*
There is a process to each of our lives and that
was part of mine.
I needed to be solitary.
I needed to dream on my own.
I needed to get used to living in my own skin
because the work that I would be doing someday
would require much courage and much confidence.
I am now doing that work
and it would have been impossible
if I had not been willing to be
The Girl Behind the Closed Door.

FREE AT LAST

When I retrieved this poem from my files, for the making of this book, I was surprised that the sentiments expressed in 1991, were very similar to those that I feel now. The difference being, of course, that in 1991 I was making my entrance back into the world after being isolated for all those years. Now, I am emerging from my silence, fear, and invisibility and going to a place where I have never been before; one that requires me to be courageous; to be as big as life; and to speak my truth.

I had to change a couple of lines, but I was amazed at the fact that I had written the line, "I see the crowd before me." I have no idea now what that would have meant to me at that time. I think it was a different kind of crowd, but I would like to think that it was a premonition of what was to come! Now, as I get up to speak to groups of people I will feel the essence of these words within me.

I also derive much strength from these words that I wrote in 1991, because in the past I have felt very frightened and very vulnerable in the business world, and thus, I stayed out of it. However, now as I choose to enter that realm, I remember the courage of that woman who consciously chose to join the real world again, and how terrifying that was for her. That woman was ME, and it is wonderful to have myself as a role model as I once again stretch the boundaries of my comfort zone.

FREE AT LAST

The gates are swinging open,
The barbed wire has lost its sting.
The chains are lying loose on the ground,
The birds feel free to sing.
I see the world before me
Just waiting with welcoming smiles.
I've waited so long for this moment,
For this, I have weathered the miles.
With baited breath I take one step,
Sounds simple, but so hard for me.
That step requires much courage,
I step past the gate and I'm free.
The birds sing out in triumph
A rainbow forms in the sky.
The four winds blow in harmony,
The sun gives a wink of his eye.
I see the crowd before me
They look so willing, so eager to learn.
I take a moment to say a short prayer.
Now I know why I had to return.

POST SCRIPT TO LINDSEY AND JASON

As I edit this book I am sad that there are no poems written to the two of you. I apologize for that. I wrote a lot about Sean because, as we all know by now, he had most of the burden of carrying me through my years of fear and depression. He was very much on my mind during my healing years, which is when I wrote most of this poetry. I often felt like I would be spending the rest of my life making up to Sean for the time he lost because of me.

Jason, you are my younger son and so you stay young in my mind. However, you have turned into a man that I am proud to know and love. You are on your own search for your purpose in life, and I love to watch you in your quest. You will find it one day and when you do, you will realize that you knew it all along! On that day, you will know peace. From the day you were born, you have delighted my heart! My prayer for you is that one day you will let us meet, once more, the boy who left us so very long ago. Be happy, Jason, and never give up the search.

Lindsey, you are the daughter I love, but the child I did not know. What a gift I received when I saw you on my doorstep that night in 1978—a beautiful 16 year old gift with a rebellious smile on her face. Since then, you have turned into a woman that I admire very much. You have put your all into raising your family, but you have saved very little for yourself. My wish for you is to one day stop and see what I see in you; your shining beauty inside and out; your value to the world; and your wonderful gifts and talents. That day will come, but only when you are ready for it, and only when you choose it.

To Alexander, Amanda, Ben, Jenna, and Ysannah: I send you my love. Fortunately, you were not witness to my sick years, either due to age or absence—that's the good news. The bad news is if you were not a part of the problem in those days, you do not get a poem! You are a part of my life now and for that I feel very blessed and I thank you for being here. I love you all very much.

MORE ABOUT THE AUTHOR

Marilyn Avient lives on Vancouver Island off the coast of British Columbia, Canada with her husband, John, and their two dogs, Ceili and Newton. They have three children and five grandchildren all of whom still live in Alberta. John is retired and, to his delight, the weather is mild enough on the Island that he can golf winter and summer. He has retired and now Marilyn is busy putting her dreams into action by writing and speaking every chance she gets.

Marilyn is using her life-long spiritual search, and her years of clinical depression, as the basis for her work. She gives keynote addresses with the intent of touching and helping at least one person in every gathering. She says that nothing feels more wonderful than looking into the eyes of audience members and meeting them, even for a second, in a place of mutual understanding and peace.

When Marilyn is not writing or speaking, she takes part in activities with her sisters in Beta Sigma Phi and spends one day a week playing Mah-jong. All of the wonderful women in these two groups helped Marilyn conquer her homesickness when she moved to the Island in 2003. The rest of the time, Marilyn and John enjoy watching movies, gardening, and playing with their cherished puppies.

OTHER BOOKS BY THE MARILYN AVIENT

Free at Last My Journey Into, Through, and Out of Depression

From Where I'm Standing (Down-to-earth spiritual workbook)

Judy's Rainbow (A child's book of learning)

A Lesson for Neddy (A wonderful lesson for all children)

www.marilynavient.com
marilynavient@shaw.ca

www.ingramcontent.com/pod-product-compliance
Lightning Source LLC
Chambersburg PA
CBHW031208270326
41931CB00006B/470